2-18-80

To Don Woods,

I wish you every good blessing in Christ.

Meyers Powell
Isa 61: 1-3

HEALING ADVENTURE

Anne S. White

Luke 4: 18-19

Also by the author:

Dayspring
Victorious Ministry
The Transforming Power of God

HEALING ADVENTURE

by

ANNE S. WHITE

LOGOS INTERNATIONAL
Plainfield, New Jersey

First Edition 1969 in England
Second Edition 1970 in England
Third Edition 1970 in Sweden
Fourth Edition 1971 in England
Logos Edition 1972 in United States

ISBN 0-912106-35-2

LOGOS International edition by arrangement with
Arthur James Ltd., Evesham, Worcs., England.

SCRIPTURE QUOTATIONS

Unless otherwise stated, Bible references are taken by kind
permission from *The New English Bible,* published by the Oxford
University Press and the Cambridge University Press, London, 1961.

LOGOS INTERNATIONAL
185 North Avenue
Plainfield, N. J. 07060
Printed in the United States of America

FOREWORD

It doesn't take a very careful inspection of the Holy Scripture to see that the Lord Jesus Christ spent a very large part of His time healing the sick. God's People today are gradually coming to realize that Jesus hasn't stopped healing, but that it is His intent that His People continue the ministry of healing, by the power of the Holy Spirit. The very word used in the New Testament for "salvation" is equally well translated "healing"; *health* and *holiness* are closely related words, and closely related ideas. God desires to save and to heal spirits, souls, and bodies.

Anne S. White has done a careful, readable, and inspiring work in presenting the meaning of healing through Christ in her book "Healing Adventure". I have personally appreciated her approach to the subject, and have enjoyed getting to know her as a friend, and having opportunity to observe her ministry. She is keenly aware that healing not only includes the physical body, but also the soul—the intellect, emotions, and will. Most important, she realizes that healing must either proceed from, or lead to, the renewing of the spirit, that perfect healing of the inward man which is the new birth, salvation through Jesus Christ.

It is good to note, though that while Mrs. White has a deep interest in the psychological aspects of Spiritual healing, she does not slip into the jargon of the psychologist, but sticks closely to the language and concepts of Holy Scripture, and of historic Christian thought.

A few really good books have been written on the subject of Christian healing during these past years. Today, when the interest in healing is strongly increasing with the wonderful renewal that is taking place throughout the Christian world, this book "Healing Adventure" will take its place as truly helpful to those who have become, or are becoming aware of this important ministry of Jesus today.

Dennis J. Bennett, B.D.
Rector of St. Luke's Episcopal Church,
Seattle, Wash.

INTRODUCTION

Everyone who is interested in divine healing should find in this book a real adventure into the field which challenges their thinking and here discover new realms for exploration. An adventure offers a challenge, an exciting undertaking. So the seeker should find in this book by Anne S. White a deepening knowledge of well-known truths and the unfolding of new light on the subject of divine healing.

The author is well qualified to write such a book. Her extensive preparation for work in counselling and ministry to the emotionally disturbed has fitted her to speak with authority on this challenging subject. Anne has given years to writing, teaching, counselling and praying in her lay ministry in churches of other denominations as well as her own. She has served as counsellor and leader of healing workshops in Camps Farthest Out and Faith-at-Work conferences. She has led Christian "Ashrams" in Norway and Sweden, missionary teaching in Japan, and Schools of Prayer in England and various cities of the United States. Wherever she has made her home, she has blended her life with that of the people of each community. Everywhere she has been active in ministering to the needs about her and has been a channel for God's healing power.

In this book Anne White not only makes clear various methods of healing contact with God through Christ Jesus but also gives specific warning of areas which may draw the seeker for healing into false paths and after spirits that are not of God. Every great reality is usually plagued by counterfeits. Jesus and Paul encountered such forces and gave clear instruction to "try the spirits, if they be of God". It is wise for us today to know those things which are of Christ and to realize He is the Truth and the Life.

The book tells many authentic stories which reveal how healings came to various persons. Mrs. White makes clear to the readers many paths they may take as they seek healing for mind, body and spirit, and she emphasizes the need of healing in every area of life.

With deep concern the author deals with the responsibility of the Christian Church today. She recalls that Jesus gave authority to those whom He sent out to spread His Gospel and that He also gave them authority to heal the sick and cast out devils. This commission is to the Christian Clergy today for Jesus gave this authority to all those who should believe on Him through these disciples.

This book is vibrant with meaning for this hour. A publisher once said to me, "One never knows when God may place His finger on a book so that it sells beyond the expectation of the author and the publisher." *Healing Adventure* may be such a book.

GENEVIEVE PARKHURST
Author and Speaker

Woodward
Oklahoma

DEDICATION

*To all those
who seek to understand and experience
more of our blessed Lord's healing Power
that to Him may be the glory!*

AUTHOR'S ACKNOWLEDGEMENTS

My gratitude is expressed to those quoted—laity, clergy and doctors—for their kind permission to use their written words to encourage those who need Christ's healing touch today. I am grateful to many who at the time of their healing gave permission to use their real-life stories to help others find God's healing love, so that the pilgrimage of life might become an Adventure with Christ. My debt is great to many prayer partners and friends, who gave lovingly of endless hours in typing, constructive criticism, editing and proof-reading of the manuscript—without whose encouragement it would never have come into being. My publisher, and many clergy and lay friends gave needed perspective and advice on final revisions of this book's fourth edition.

I thank God for giving me my husband, our daughter and our son who shared with me in this Healing Adventure with Christ. Lastly, I give thanks for three who are now in the Larger Life: my loving parents, whose encouragement and prayers led me to write; and my English prayer partner, Joan Ritchie, whose friendship made more meaningful the English chapter of our life.

ANNE S. WHITE

Winter Park
Florida 32789.

CONTENTS

I

MY FIRST ENCOUNTER

For three long years our five-year-old son had suffered from dreadful asthmatic attacks, and even a change of climate had brought no relief. During the most severe times of congestion, he had to be given shots of adrenalin to relieve his labored breathing. My heart sank as I heard our son's pediatrician say: "There's not much hope that he will outgrow this, although he might in about seven years. We've tried all the wonder drugs. There's really nothing more we can do medically." It seemed to me that I could not bear such a verdict, for already the child was almost a hypochondriac and I dreaded each interminable heart-breaking spell. Somehow I felt guilty.

That night as I put out the light, it seemed that my childhood faith (which I had lost at college) was restored, for I had just read of many recent healings to God's glory. Strangely enough, most of them involved resentments and the need for forgiveness of this sin of the heart. At two in the morning I awakened and went to see what I could do to relieve our son's labored breathing, but it was too early to give any medicine. Inwardly, as I groaned "There's nothing I can do", I sensed a still small voice within me saying, "Yes, there is. You can kneel down and pray." In amazement I heard this quiet assurance within me: "It is not My Will for an innocent child to suffer. It is your bitter resentment and you must forgive this person." By God's grace I was able to say, "I forgive her, Lord"—and to my great surprise I really meant it! The still small voice continued, "If you *really* have faith you will thank Me before you see the results." And in that moment of amazing grace, I heard myself saying, "Thank you, Lord." Our son took one deep, quiet breath—

and he has never had another asthmatic attack!

Thus began my healing adventure—an adventure with God, seeking to know more of His Will; to practice more of the principles of prayer which our Lord taught in His earthly ministry; to follow Him. This has revolutionized my attitude toward God and toward my family and those about me. As a laywoman I have sought to be used to channel His healing Love and Power into the lives of those whom He has brought into my life, not because I am worthy, but because *He* is worthy. I have seen His Love heal those bruised by the sin of the world; those filled with hate (as I once was); those victims of their own self-pity—the bitter, the fearful.

This healing adventure which was begun twenty-five years ago has involved me in the ministry of intercessory prayer in many different countries as far apart as Japan, England, Scandinavia and the Holy Land, as well as in many parts of America. Always our blessed Lord has revealed His healing Love. He is no respecter of persons, only conditions. The searching of the Scriptures has convinced me that in healing the sick, our Lord was proclaiming the Will of God; that it is a human "No" rather more often than God's "No". To be divinely healed means to surrender to God. For many this price is too great, too costly. For many it is too hard to break free from the coddling of illness and assume full responsibility for life once more. For many it is easier to take a pill than to give up a life-long habit, grudge, resentment or fear. But after having witnessed the miracles of the healing Love of Christ in my own life and those with whom our Lord has led me to pray, I am convinced that when we as the Body of Christ, the Church, provide a real climate of faith, His touch will have its ancient power!

Twenty-five hundred years ago Hippocrates so wisely suggested treating the whole man. Later Plato said that one ought not to neglect the healing of the soul when making the effort to cure the body. We can be thankful for doctors both in England and America who have many centuries later confirmed the interaction between spirit, mind, body and soul—the relationships exemplified by our Lord in His earthly ministry of healing. We can be especially grateful for those doctors who pray with their patients or meet regularly with pastors to share the healing work of ministering to the whole man. A study of their writings points to the important part played by human emotions on the body. It is hoped that this book will help to relate the approach of psychosomatic medicine to our Lord's healing ministry: that which is taking place today through His Body the Church as well as during the visible ministry of Jesus of Nazareth.

Now, as then, the healing of the spirit and soul is integrated with the healing of the body and mind. With only a few exceptions the healings described within these pages have been related from my intimate knowledge of the persons involved although names have been changed. In almost all cases, medical records have stood behind the diagnoses described; in almost all cases, the one healed has become a channel of God's power to others, in gratitude for what He has done. It is to be hoped that these words may challenge readers to try out for themselves in the "laboratory of life", in deep prayers of faith, the principles illustrated in Holy Scriptures, corroborated by Christian doctors and practiced in these examples of Christian healing today. It may be that when our Lord finds a true climate of faith again restored to His Church, we may cease to be like Nazareth where "he did not work many miracles there: such was their want of faith" (Matthew 13:58). When the healing ministry is proclaimed in every Church, the name of Jesus Christ will be more glorified than when some theologians seek to proclaim that "God is Dead"! For when one has been touched and healed by the Living God there is no argument that can alter the faith that Jesus Christ is with us "always, to the end of time" (Matthew 28:20).

It has been said that "one person practicing the truth of Christ's teachings is worth ten thousand recitings of the words". In his address, Dr. T. F. Davey challenged Christian medical workers at the Tubingen Conference sponsored by the Department of World Mission and Evangelism of the World Council of Churches and the Lutheran World Federation. He pointed out that every person who is a part of the Body of Christ can receive the renewal of His indwelling Life, and that we are called as Christians to share His creative energy with others. He quoted from St. Teresa's letter to her minister: "Christ has no body now on earth but yours, no hands but yours, no feet but yours. It is through your eyes that he must look out in mercy on the world. He needs your feet to go about doing good. Yours must be his hands raised to bless."[1]

The healing Christ is not the Christ who is generally known today and yet He is the Christ who will redeem the world. He comes silently into the hearts of those who love Him, touching them through their infirmities and healing them through their afflictions. The healing Christ is not the Christ who is generally preached today. He is relegated by many to the state of "myth", or at best He belongs in the eyes of many to the Apostolic Age alone. The healing Christ is not the Christ who is generally worshipped today, for He has been shrouded in a web of doctrinal arguments and ritualistic services—not that He cannot be the center of all doctrines and rituals when unbound by the finiteness of man's mind! The healing Christ is not the Christ who is generally proclaimed in the life of His Church today—yet only He can heal its mighty divisions and bring to its multiplicity the unity of His Body. The healing Christ is not the Christ who is looked to for the salvation of the world today— yet only He who was in the foundation of the world, who died for its sins, can save it by the power of His healing Love released throughout all its lands. The healing Christ has come to bring Life—and to bring it more abundantly!

May the stricken and sin-sick world about us be able to see in the lives of Christians the only sermons it is apt to hear. May our lives proclaim victorious living, the healing of broken minds, bodies, spirits and souls; and the restoring of broken relationships by the mercy and grace of our Risen Lord (Luke 10:27-28).

II

WHAT IS DIVINE HEALING?

In my earnest search to learn more of "the how of healing", I began to study the Scriptures and to read the experiences and conclusions of those who were pioneering the restoration of the healing ministry to the Church. As in the case of my child, Divine Healing is the gift of God to the sufferer in need. The healing of the mind and body are earnestly to be prayed for; but the healing of the spirit and soul are even more important. In this instance, my own spiritual healing of resentment and fear led me to begin my healing adventure with Jesus.

In our world of broken relationships, which one of us does not need healing of the total personality? Divine Healing is now being restored to the Church's ministry; but it is as old as the Gospels. Although it seems too good to be true, it is simply taking Jesus at His word, accepting His interpretation of God's Will for us to be made whole in mind and body as well as in soul and spirit. Divine Healing is allowing God to use our faith and love to accomplish His *perfect* Will in us and in others. Thus we see that it is a matter of aligning oneself with the perfect Will of God, so that "the God who raised Christ Jesus from the dead will also give new life to your mortal bodies through his indwelling Spirit" (Romans 8:11). We accept this healing in whatever way, place and time He chooses.

God is the Healer but He may use us as His channels for His re-creating Power and Love. In subsequent chapters we shall see that He may heal directly through our prayers as the faithful believers and the sacraments of the Church; or He may use doctors and *materia medica* as His instruments of healing. Our healing may, in fact, come through any one or a combination of several ways, according to His choice. The pity is that our healing may also be limited by our capacity and willingness to surrender ourselves to God and to receive what God is so willing and waiting to give! Inasmuch as God Himself has given us freedom of will to reject or accept His Will in whole or in part, so He has in fact limited Himself in His operation within our lives.

It is well known to doctors that they can set the climate for healing but they cannot force the human body to heal. It is so created that the power of the patient's mind and will can work either for or against healing. If the patient is determined to live, the doctor has a strong ally in the healing of the patient's body. The will, the deep motive, the burning desire of the patient has a very noticeable power over the cells and tissues, although it is not the only factor, of course. Similarly, if the patient is determined to die, his mind can greatly influence the outcome, vastly hindering the work of medicine. This fact is recorded by Dr. Loring T. Swaim in his excellent book *Arthritis, Medicine and the Spiritual Laws.*

A few years ago while visiting a distant city where I had spoken on the Will of God to heal, a friend asked me to visit a woman in hospital. The doctors had said that the only thing hindering this patient's recovery was her lack of will to live; and that without this, she was in critical condition, for there was nothing more they could do. My friend and I saw the woman the next day. We had prayed in the car before entering the hospital that our Lord would Himself prepare the way in the patient's heart and give us His words to say to her: words that would quicken her faith and convey to her His Love, not just our human love.

We witnessed to her quietly of God's transforming power in healing my son of a malignancy (see page 85). We assured her that God was no respecter of persons but loved all of His children equally. Her closed, discouraged mind seemed to open to the Good News that God loved her and had a plan and purpose for her life. Then we asked the Lord to pray through us the prayer that would unlock the door in her subconscious mind as well as in her conscious mind. The words were of promise and thanksgiving that He had healed her for a purpose which He would unfold beginning at that moment and continuing like the opening of the petals of a rose. As we quietly removed our hands from her head, there seemed to be a new glow in her eyes. She agreed to read my earlier book, *The Transforming Power of God,* and to pray each day for God to heal her, to guide and bless her, to fill and use her "according to His perfect plan for her life". We promised to lift her to the Lord throughout the days ahead in thanksgiving for His "healing of the will" which had now begun in her. Within a few days she was able to leave the hospital. Later she wrote that she went home a new person in Christ Jesus, with a new purpose, a new will to live to glorify Him. This was a double healing: for the friend who brought a woman to Christ on the strength of her own then shaky faith felt a new purpose come into her own life as well.

Divine Healing is much more than "getting well"; it is indeed being made whole. It is healing not only of the symptoms but also of the causes of disease. It concerns the healing of our emotions and will as well as our ailments; therefore it concerns our relationships with our God and our neighbor. In Luke 10:27-28, we read: "You shall love the Lord your God with all your heart, and with all your soul, and with all your strength, and with all your mind; and your neighbor as yourself." And he said to him, "You have answered right; do this, and you will live." We need today to heed these words. It means that God (who created us) knows far better than we our need for integration; and, in touching us with His healing power, He releases within us His new Life, permeating our entire being, making us more effective instruments of His Will. This was a vital part of the earthly ministry of Jesus Christ. It was in fact the continuing faith of the Early Christian Church. Those who look askance today at the healing ministry might well be reminded that it is only a restoration of the work carried on by the apostles and their successors for several centuries. Those who seek revival in the Church today might well consider this part of the total Gospel which has failed to be proclaimed in the intervening centuries.

Divine Healing is centered in the Atonement—in Jesus Christ, the Saviour, Healer, Redeemer of mankind. His sacrifice for the redemption of human sin enables man to be spiritually healed by the acceptance of His forgiving Love. Jesus identified Himself with the whole human race in becoming man, in accepting John's baptism, and in submitting to the wrath of jealous men who put Him to death on the Cross. When He rose again, He released a new power to overcome sin. He bears our suffering with us when we offer it to Him.

We use the term "Divine Healing" to avoid confusion. "Spiritual healing" can be misunderstood to mean Spiritualism. "Christian healing" is often confused with "Christian Science". "Faith healing" can suggest healing on the lower psychic levels of personal magnetism, hypnosis, auto-suggestion, and so on. Therefore, we must distinguish between "Divine Healing" as we mean it, and these other ways and methods.

Although notable cures have been effected through Spiritualism, Christian Science and "faith healing" cults whose first concern is to heal the body, they cannot fully claim to be rooted and grounded in the redeeming Love of Jesus Christ who died to *save* us. Through His forgiveness of sin and empowering Holy Spirit, the sick are healed in mind, body, soul and spirit—bringing true wholeness and integration. Spiritualism claims to heal with the supposed aid of spirits of the dead whereas the Scriptures forbid attempts to contact them. Anyone who reads Isaiah 8:19 can see that this is a sin: therefore, whoever is guilty of this disobedience should ask God's forgiveness and then renounce any such contact with evil before claiming the cleansing power of Jesus' Blood over the whole experience. In Hebrews 9:27 we read: "It is appointed for men to die once, and after that comes judgment". Satan is known as the "deceiver of the brethren", and he can impersonate and even heal to suit his own ends. St. Paul cast out the "spirit of divination" (an evil spirit) from the slave girl who had been telling fortunes—and she lost her power: we can see rather clearly its source (Acts 16:16-18; RSV). If any reader has dabbled in books of magic, it is wise and Scriptural to burn them (Acts 18:18-19). Divine Healing calls only upon the third person of the Trinity, the Holy Spirit. It is always safe to open ourselves to His inspiration (inflowing Spirit) for He is the Holy Comforter whom Jesus promised to send to lead us into all Truth; but it is very dangerous to open ourselves to the psychic realm of the occult where invasion by evil spirits is extremely likely. A psychic door in one's life should be guarded by the Cross of Christ: that is the sign we claim (not the signs of the zodiac!) Mediums, "guides", seances, ouija boards should be avoided because they are forbidden by Scripture. "Automatic writing" is equally dangerous. I have prayed with many people who have been released by the Lord gloriously from occult involvements. Ignorance is neither an excuse nor a protection; obedience to the Word of God is imperative. For a more detailed explanation, please read carefully the very clear warnings in Chapter 4 of *The Holy Spirit and You* by Dennis and Rita Bennett.[1]

Christian Science is based on the theory that sin and evil are not reality; if this were true, we would not need a Savior! Hence they deny the need of the Atonement. Healing becomes more the result of man's will to think positively and pull himself up by his own bootstraps. "Faith healing" is dependent upon the ability of the patient himself (or of the so-called "healer") to force a consciousness of healing upon the sick person's subconscious and conscious mind. Even if he succeeds, there is the probability of recurrent outbreaks of the same or associated disease after a brief remission unless the deep-rooted cause in the patient is removed or healed.

Only God can forgive sin and heal the sense of guilt which is often the root of *dis*-ease! Our faith in Divine Healing is in Jesus, not in any human being or group or even in prayer *per se,* although all of.them may be necessary channels or vehicles of His Power. Our faith is in Jesus Christ whose Love, Forgiveness and Healing Grace flow through many channels, creatively renewing life not just for the favored minority but for all of humanity. True, this is accelerated in those who meet Jesus' condition of expectant faith: "Whatever you ask for in prayer, believe that you have received it and it will be yours" (Mark 11:24).

Experiments have proved that a person who is hypnotized will burn at the exact point where a pen touches his skin if he is assured that this contact is with a hot iron. Even Pavlov's experiment with dogs proved that the body functions according to recognized stimuli. After repeated experiences of associating a certain noise (the ringing of a bell, for instance) with its mealtime, it was found that at the sound of the bell, the animal's mouth would water and his digestive system would begin to prepare for the food it was accustomed to receive.

The power of the mind is medically accepted as a channel either for healing or for disease. A very wise doctor said to a woman who had come to him complaining of having the symptoms of multiple sclerosis, "What is it that you don't want to do?" The woman faced honestly the duty she was dreading, realizing that this disease was far worse than the responsibility that she feared and resented; and she never contracted multiple sclerosis! In *Arthritis, Medicine and the Spiritual Laws,* Dr. Loring T. Swaim confirms what I discovered in praying for others as well as myself: that the subconscious mind often creates illness as a result of emotions sometimes unbeknown to us. A desire to avoid a duty (or perhaps to be noticed) may be fulfilled by an ailment that makes itself our valid excuse. But if we continue indefinitely in great tension, the functional illness can become organic.

If the human mind can so influence and control the body, then a Higher Influence brought to bear on the individual's mind can be a means of healing the body. God has so created man that his spirit can be interpenetrated and directed by the Holy Spirit. When so attuned, man's spirit dominates the soul which is said to be the center of our emotions, desires and demands for self-gratification. As we shall see later, these emotions and desires have a strong influence on bodily health. Wholeness of personality depends largely on this relationship in which the Holy Spirit indwells the human spirit as Senior Partner and thus integrates all of one's being—spirit, soul, mind and body. When the spirit is out of relationship with God (that is, estranged by such emotions as guilt, fear, resentment, self-pity, jealousy or pride) the natural healing processes of the body are impaired. The body's cells are constantly being recreated. A broken bone will knit even if it is not set by a doctor; it is the *vis medicatrix naturae,* that God-given power of recuperation that is implanted in every human being, which brings about the healing.

Ben, a twelve-year-old boy, broke his leg while riding a "skate-board" in the street. As a truck came around the corner unexpectedly, he swerved into the concrete curb to avoid being struck. His remorse was the greater because he had disobeyed his parents. The thought of being immobilized in a heavy cast for nine weeks only aggravated the pain. His mother wisely explained that God had not punished him; but that although he had broken his leg in disobedience, God's forgiveness and healing power would flow into him—through his own prayers as well as those of his parents and friends. On the day he felt the most pain and discomfort, his minister came to have a prayer with him. To Ben's surprise, the pain left him and he had more faith to pray for himself. He was able to forgive himself because he realized that God and his parents had forgiven him. For eight long weeks he studied hard to keep up with his class. To Ben's joy he could celebrate his thirteenth birthday without the cast. It had come off a week earlier than the doctor had expected and his leg was straight and normal. When report cards came out, Ben had made all A's and B's! A year later he won his track event at school. God's healing power through the doctor's help had restored his leg perfectly.

Under the direction of the doctor, much can be done to assist the body in the working of its natural machinery and to counteract adverse conditions and influences. Under the direction of the Holy Spirit, the spirit, soul and mind of the patient can also be harnessed in the effort of healing, but only if the patient believes it is God's Will to heal. If the sick man does not believe it is God's Will for his strength to be restored, for example, he will not fully cooperate in his innermost being with the doctor's efforts or with the latent natural powers in his body. A block of doubt is set in the channel for healing; and it is the work of Divine Healing through the Church to help to remove this block. This cannot be done by the prayer, *"If* it be Thy Will." The sick man's subconscious mind accepts the "if" and is left with an indecisive response. A wavering doubt creeps into the deeper consciousness and it is reflected in the body in a negative response. In fact, many a doctor has been aware of deterioration in his patient's condition after such a prayer. A man who was recovering from a critical heart attack suffered a temporary set-back immediately after a minister prayed a prayer of doubt rather than of faith. On the other hand, in the case of another critically ill heart patient, the prayer of faith was the channel the Lord used to effect a temporary healing in a man who had been an avowed agnostic. Although the patient died a few months later, his conversion to the Lord was glorious!

In conclusion, let us now re-emphasize that God the Creator has a purpose for each of us and He is concerned with the whole person—spirit, mind, soul and body—the totality of our being. As we become aware of His healing Power and live in obedience to His Will, He integrates and heals.

III

GOD'S WILL

As a one-time "intellectual skeptic" I found it necessary to come through a study of Scripture and much prayer until the Lord guided me to the understanding shared here. To me this is fundamental—for unless God wills healing, it is useless for me to pray for it. It makes no sense to pray one way with our lips and hold a contrary belief in our subconscious minds, hearts or intellects. What I had seen in the experience of healing needed confirmation in my intellect. The Lord led me through many books and many speakers until my intellect was converted from its doubts. In my lay ministry of prayer-counselling I have found that these answers which helped me have been meaningful to others also.

The Nature of God

Is sickness the Will of God? When a man struggling with emphysema asked me this question I reminded him that Jesus described God as a loving Father who will not give us a stone when we ask for bread. The sick man had a most confused picture because he had listened to the many Christians who quickly ascribe calamities as being "sent by the Will of God", while in the next breath they call Him their Heavenly Father. To say that God allows man freedom of will is not to say that He wills its misuse. God permits sickness, accidents and war but He does not intentionally will or cause them. He has to allow man freedom of will or else there would be no true love—it would be coerced. Yet God is always working patiently within circumstances to draw man to voluntary acceptance of His Love and of His higher intentional Will. He uses our prayers of love and faith as instruments to bring about His ultimate Will.

A six-year-old child was told repeatedly after the accidental death of her beloved father, "It was God's Will, so you must just accept it." Finally in despair she burst out, "Then I hate God!" How could she love a God who was cruel enough to take from her life the loving father whom she so badly needed and so greatly missed? Such a shortsighted explanation may be the reason why many today hold a resentment against God. It is poor theology to explain in this way an airplane crash which was in fact caused by human carelessness or mechanical failure. A friend reading this manuscript commented that as a child she had heard that her father's death was "God's will"—and she carried a resentment against God until at thirty-five she found Him as her loving Heavenly Father.

God allows illness but He does not send or inflict it. Job's friends indicated a prevalent Jewish belief that sickness was a mark of God's displeasure and that health was a clear sign of His favor. But Job said that the thing he feared had come upon him (Job 3:25). The Jews asked Jesus whose sin (the man's or his parents') had caused him to be born blind (John 9:1-4). They indicated their belief that affliction or disease was God's punishment for sin, but Jesus replied that the man's suffering was not sent by God to "chastise" him. This belief that God chastises is reflected in many of the Psalms but in Psalm 103:2-3 we read: "Bless the Lord, O my soul, and forget not all his benefits: who forgiveth all thine iniquities; who healeth all thy diseases" (KJV).

When a little child in ignorance puts his hand on the hot stove he is burned, not because God is seeking to chastise him, but because a physical law of heat has caused this effect. If it were truly God's intentional Will to punish an innocent child, He could hardly be called the loving Heavenly Father and Giver of good gifts!

Could we ever conceive of God looking through a list of suitable diseases to ascertain which would be fixed on one of His so-called beloved children? No earthly father would deliberately will his son to be an imbecile or to be tortured by epilepsy or cancer. How can anyone ever attribute such a sinister will to our Heavenly Father? In Matthew's Gospel,

Jesus is recorded as having said: "If you, then, bad as you are, know how to give your children what is good for them, how much more will your heavenly Father give good things to those who ask him!" (7:11).

Jesus Is God Incarnate

Set beside this the very clear Gospel pictures of Jesus, healing the sick of *every* known disease. Surely our Lord was not interfering with God's purposes or working contrary to the Will of His Father in heaven. His healings were certainly too numerous to be mere exaggerations. He deliberately and ruthlessly attacked the causes of disease whether they were of physical or spiritual origin. Never did He tell any sick person that it was good for him to bear his suffering or that it was God's Will for him to suffer. On the contrary, Jesus healed them, *every one.* Consider the case of the leper, who, bowing to the ground, begged: "Sir, . . . if only you will, you can cleanse me." The leper was instantly healed. And many in the crowds that gathered to hear Jesus were cured of their illnesses (Luke 5:12-15). Is it so impossible to believe that a leper can be healed by the touch of our Lord? Will it not be rather difficult to explain away the Gospel accounts of His healing ministry inasmuch as they comprise two thirds of the records of His life, excluding the events of the Last Week? If we try to dismiss them, we shall find ourselves with very little left.

If It Be Thy Will

At no time did Jesus or His disciples pray a prayer of "If it be Thy Will" *in connection with healing.* As we said previously, this clause in the Garden of Gethsemane was *not* a prayer of *healing.* It was quite clearly a prayer of *guidance* and *commitment.* Jesus prayed to know if He was to go through the experience of the Cross, or if God had some other plan for the deliverance of mankind. The redemption of the world was the task to which Jesus was committed. He was praying for His Father's guidance in that last hour, and for strength to enable Him to go through the experience of the

Cross. The prayer of guidance should always be a request for the clarification of God's Will. The prayer of healing should always be prayed in the certainty of God's Will for *healing and wholeness* as demonstrated unmistakably in the earthly ministry and teachings of our Lord! The prayer for salvation of a soul (the main object of healing) should be prayed in the same certainty of God's Will. The fact that freedom of will enables us to resist God's intentional Will for our salvation does not change our assurance that such is His Will. Neither should the failure of a person to be healed change our confidence in wholeness as the intentional Will of God. I have found it is better to pray "according to Thy Perfect Plan, Lord".

To many this concept that healing (wholeness) is the Will of God may seem too radical—because in Medieval times the "If it be Thy Will" clause became well entrenched in the prayers of the Church, lingering to the present in some churches. That this was not always so can be proved by a study of prayers of faith handed down from the Early Christian Church. While living in London, I found a book by the English layman who pioneered the modern restoration of the healing ministry in both England and America. He wrote that about 1000 A.D. a monk named Reginald inserted this clause as he copied the prayers of ages past. It was easier for the Church of that day to cover failures with this clause than to admit lack of faith in God's healing power. As we shall see in more detail in our next chapter, Jesus healed *all* who were brought to Him—individually and in multitudes: the lame, the blind, the deaf, the demented, the paralyzed, the lepers, the sick of varying diseases.

Only in Nazareth does the Biblical account indicate some limitation: "He could work no miracle there, except that he put his hands on a few sick people and healed them; and he was taken aback by their want of faith" (Mark 6:5, 6). If even Jesus was "taken aback" and "could work no miracle there" because of "their want of faith", then isn't our "want of faith" a very important deterrent to the healing Will of God today? Obviously, Jesus was *not* disobeying the Will of His Father in healing the sick! He asserted, "I have come down from heaven, not to do my own will, but the will of

him who sent me" (John 6:38). And on the Mount of Trans- ✓
figuration His Father's voice was heard: "This is my Son, my
Chosen; listen to him" (Luke 9:35).

Are we listening to Him today—or to our own inner voices
of doubt and fear of failure? We˙say in fear, "What if the
person we have earnestly prayed for should not recover?"
This is no more a proof of God's Will to withhold healing
than is the failure of the sinner to be converted a proof that
God does not want to save souls. We have not yet fully
learned the lessons Jesus taught of the spiritual principles (or
laws) of faith, love, surrender, thanksgiving, humility. Later
we shall see the importance in real life situations of spiritual
laws that can supersede natural laws—when they are *lived,*
not just talked about! We are to co-operate, to be co-workers
with God, as He works out His Plan!

An airplane is held to the earth by gravity, an unchanging
law; but it is lifted to the skies by the application of another
law. Yet we do not say that the law of gravity has been
broken. It has been superseded. Although we are (or should
be) always aware that our prime concern is with the spirit
designed for eternal life, we have every reason to believe that
Christ meant us to obey these "spiritual laws" so that our
bodies may be capable of a *maximum vocation* in His service,
remembering that we are to be the temples of His Holy
Spirit.

Developing Character

Some say that physical suffering and disease are intentionally sent by God for "purification of the soul" or "develop-
ing character" If this were true, then the victim would have
no right as a Christian to seek relief through medicine, for
this would be thwarting the alleged "Will of God"! Indeed, if
such were the case, doctors, nurses and all who engage in
medical research for alleviation and cure of disease would be
sinners since they would be aiding the victims of God's
alleged Will to escape from its rigors. It is appalling that
many intelligent and devout Christians believe such rubbish.
The pity is that so many sick persons in need of their prayers
for healing and wholeness are denied this most necessary

help. Poor logic and lack of faith masquerade behind this travesty of the clearly instructed and demonstrated Will of God, as manifested in both the teachings and actions of Jesus Christ, His Son, our Lord.

Incurable Disease

When a doctor says a cancer is incurable, he really means that to date science has not found an absolute cure in the realm of *materia medica* although surgery, radium, medicines and deep-ray therapy are found to be useful treatments. If Jesus could heal "incurable" leprosy during His earthly ministry, can He not heal, for example, cancerous cells of modern times with the spiritual "radium", the deep-ray therapy of His Love? The late Dr. Griffith Evans, a distinguished London physician, made a detailed study of cancer patients whom he had treated. In his booklet, *Cancer,* he wrote: "I am convinced that the disturbed and strained emotions are the exciting causes of the cancers. . . . What has the Christian faith to offer in these circumstances? It offers an immediate change of heart, conversion or salvation. It offers the resources of infinite, ambient, benevolent energy which enters the body through channels provided. The reinforcement [of the immune reaction] depends on belief."[1]

If a cause of cancer is an emotional shock of great magnitude that was not spiritually resolved, is it too much to believe that healing of that deeper hurt can come as the inflow of Jesus' Love is accepted by the patient in joyous thanksgiving? Such an "emotional shock" of a very positive nature apparently reverses the body's processes, because the spiritual change has reversed the mind's and soul's reactions to the original cause. The fact is that cancer has been healed over and over again, and thousands of cases are now on record.

Dr. Alexis Carrel, a winner of the Nobel Prize for Medicine and a world-renowned pioneer in cancer research, saw a skin cancer shrivel to a scar. In his booklet called *Prayer Is Power* he said, "Prayer is a force as real as terrestrial gravity. As a physician, I have seen men, after all other therapy had failed, lifted out of disease and melancholy by the serene effort of prayer. It is the only power in the world that seems to overcome the so-called 'laws of nature' . . . Prayer is a mature activity indispensable to the fullest development of personality. . . In asking, our human deficiencies are filled and we arise strengthened and repaired."[2]

Healing Climate of Faith

Some doctors do seem to dodge the fact of God's healing by claiming a wrong diagnosis in spite of X-rays and other proofs. One marvels that they would prefer to blame themselves rather than acclaim the wonder of God; but such is the climate of the modern Nazareth! Is it a surprise that more healings are not taking place when patients are surrounded with such lack of faith? The Lord has led me to know (personally or through books) many fine, humble Christian doctors who work consciously as channels of faith as well as diagnosticians, analysts, dispensers of medicine and surgeons. Thanks be to God for their witness!

The "climate of doubt and unbelief" which surrounds many patients is not always to be laid at the doctor's door. It may well be in the family of the one so greatly in need of a "climate of faith". It is often in the very place where the sick used to come for healing—the Church itself. A friend who had been healed of cancer asked, "Why is it that I feel worse every time I go to the meeting of my circle at church?" Why, indeed! Because the Church for the most part today has left the Healing Lord on the shores of Galilee instead of inviting Him into every part of its ministry. In too many cases the Church has been trying to do the work of Christ without prayer and Bible study that would enable His healing power to flow freely into every need. We cannot do His work without the Lord Himself. But is He really the *Lord* of every Church meeting? Are the sick lifted to God in prayers of *faith* that His Grace will work through the natural recuperative powers (the "immune reaction") of the patient's body and through the wisdom and skill of the doctors and nurses who strive to be channels of healing? Or is there a kind of gossipy, negative pity (a spirit of hopelessness) projected upon the one who is in an already weakened condition? And all this in the name of "God's Will"!

Bearing the Cross

"This is her Cross" is often piously said. It seems absurd to identify arthritis with the Cross of Jesus who healed the paralytics of His day and in one case clearly set free (to use His words) the "woman whom Satan bound" (Luke 13:16 RSV). In other words, Jesus said that disease is part of the work of Satan and the sin of the world. Are we the Church following in the footsteps of our Master, waging the fight to deliver sufferers from it? In many cases (including my own) it has been found that a critical, self-righteous spirit was reflected in the rigidity of the body; and that humility, confession and deeply experienced thanksgiving opened the way to instantaneous healing of medically diagnosed arthritis. My doctor had told me that it would never get any better but rather would grow worse in time.

The Cross of Jesus was never His own physical suffering, for Jesus was never sick. The Cross He bore was the sin of the world, and the Cross He admonished His followers to bear was Christian suffering, i.e., suffering that results from the sin of the world. The wife of an alcoholic bears suffering that is the result of her husband's misuse of his body, money and time. Sadly enough, the shame that often the world inflicts upon her is an added part of its sin. If she bears this redemptively and cheerfully, loving and forgiving in the Name of Jesus, she is bearing His Cross, but not if she is a whining, self-pitying and nagging "martyr".

If a man is nagged and persecuted by his wife because of his faith—especially the time, money and love given in His Lord's service—he, too, is bearing the Cross. The wife's sins of unbelief and self-centeredness are part of the sin of the world.

A minister may make himself unpopular with members of his congregation (even risking his own dismissal) because he will not allow them to whittle the Church's ministry down to their own proportions, or limit God's Love to the size of their prejudices. He, too, is bearing the Cross. Someone once said, "Too many people have roast preacher for their Sunday dinner."

A young person, refusing to join the crowd in something that he knows to be wrong, incurs their jeers and ostracism, thus bearing the Cross. He, too, is witnessing for Christ in difficult or dangerous situations where he could more easily yield to the pressure of others. That—not arthritis or asthma—is Christian suffering! It is the kind of suffering that is voluntarily accepted when it could be evaded. Such suffering—lifted to Christ to be used to extend His redemptive work in the world—is true "bearing the Cross"

Obviously, any kind of suffering (physical because of disease, or "bearing the Cross for the sins of others") may be used by God to develop patience, gentleness and many other fruit of the Spirit. Unfortunately, physical suffering seems more often to develop bitterness. But to say that God can and does bring forth the fruit of the Spirit, that He does bring good out of evil, is *not* to say that God *intentionally wills* the suffering! As St. Paul says in his Letter to the Romans, "We know that in *everything* God works for good with those who love him, who are called according to his purpose" (8:28, RSV, italics mine).

The Thorn in the Flesh

Finally, we come to St. Paul's now famous "thorn in the flesh" behind which I have found many hide in defence of their "faith" that disease is God's intentional Will. I believe that the words refer to a harassing opponent in the sense that they appear in the Old Testament and in modern usage. Preceding St. Paul on his journeys a silversmith named Demetrius deliberately stirred up trouble for him. Others say that the "thorn" referred to a nagging wife. St. Paul himself described it as "Satan's messenger to bruise me" (II Corinthians 12:7-10). Then how could it be a visitation by God? If it were punishment for the sin of spiritual pride, we wonder why St. Paul himself claimed it to be sent ("messenger") of Satan.

My feeling is that St. Paul prayed only three times for its removal and thus failed to obey the teachings of our Lord who gave us two parables to emphasize the importance of persistency in prayer (Luke 18:1-8; Luke 11:5-10). Indeed, Jesus made the Canaanite woman wait until she persevered in prayer for the healing of her child—probably to show that God allows a testing of human faith (Matthew 15:22-28). My inference is that St. Paul should have prayed more than three times. Some of us have patiently prayed *many years* for the victories God has finally been able to work in our lives—and during the long, painful interim, His Grace has been sufficient for us! *In our weakness His Strength has been perfected while the situation was being healed.*

Throughout the Book of Acts and St. Paul's Epistles we see him as the survivor of severe beatings, scourgings and stonings that would have killed him but for the Grace of God (II Corinthians 11:23-29). He was healed also of an Asian fever and a poisonous snake bite at Malta—to say nothing of the great miracle of the healing of his sight in which Ananias was the Lord's channel.

Conditions for Healing

Often we are too busy with our petty pursuits to become aware of the fullness of God's Love and the transforming Power of Jesus. Consciously or unconsciously, we may have broken the spiritual and physical (natural) laws of the universe. Illness makes us stop and face our need. In this time of suffering we may learn needed lessons and thus find the pearl of great price. The Kingdom of God may be implanted within our hearts with such resultant Peace and Joy, such a sense of loving and being loved, that we may be able to thank God—not that He *sent* the suffering (for He did not)—but that He has brought such a blessing out of it! Acknowledging our own responsibility of guilt; forgiving that which is the result of the sins of others; finding the Presence of God and practicing this in our daily living—we become spiritually and physically healed.

The transformation of "rebirth" that takes place in such a life is radical because the whole principle becomes one's vital awareness of eternal life beginning *now* with a regenerating effect upon body and mind as the spirit and soul respond to the Love of God. This new life, like that of the first Christians, must be nourished by fellowship in sacrament, Bible study and prayer (Acts 2:42).

Usually when this change of center truly happens, a person experiences both physical and mental healing. But in some cases the physical healing does not follow as one would hope or expect. Sometimes when it appears to our human eyes that the climate for healing is ripe and that the patient and human channels have made every possible effort, the answer apparent is not the one we feel is truly God's Will. In these cases we must trust (as doctors do) that some day we shall understand better. We shall see more clearly when we see Him face to face!

Has God changed His mind from the promises He gave us so clearly through His Son, Jesus Christ? Or is it rather that some condition of healing (as yet unrecognized) has not been met—very possibly that the Body of Christ, the Church, is too divided, too weak in its faith? Will the Church be only a trickle, or will it become the stream of Living Water, a River of Healing, from which sufferers may drink? Where the Church (laity as well as clergy) offers itself in real faith as a channel of God's healing power, many people are wonderfully healed to glorify Him in radiant and consecrated lives. This proves that the gift of healing through the Church is not limited to the Apostolic Age. A marked and undeniable revival or restoration of the healing ministry is taking place in churches of many denominations and in countries round the world. The common denominator seems to be faith in God's healing power and love of Him and of all His children.

God moves wherever humility allows Him to take over in human life, but as yet the majority of Christians seem to know nothing of His Holy Spirit and care even less. There are many who are concerned with buildings, bazaars and the like. But how few belong to a Prayer Group or go to pray with the sick or visit them in hospital! Many are not healed because they lack spiritual support needed for their physical healing. When the patient has been prayed for in faith and has known this and accepted our Lord, spiritual blessing has come.

A Christian Attitude Towards Death

At a Christian Ashram I led in Sweden a miracle happened in the heart of a thirty-seven-year-old missionary just returned from Africa where his young wife had died of heart trouble, leaving him heartbroken, bereft, bitter and confused, with three little children to rear alone. God opened his eyes to see and forgive the climate of unbelief that had blocked His true Will. At our healing service he took the laying-on of hands, asking for the "transforming power of God", for strength to go on in his ministry and bring up his little ones. Next day he drove me to the station, and we prayed in his car. He was radiant as he waved goodbye using our "three-fingered Ashram greeting", meaning "Jesus is Lord!" To his friends in Africa he wrote, "I have sensed the victory that we all can have through our faith. Today it is marvelous to live through Jesus and know that the tomorrows will be just as wonderful in His company. Is it strange that it has become so natural for me to pray more, especially for others, and to seek God's Will? . . . God used the Ashram experience to make me whole again, trustful that He will provide for all our needs, and sure that He will have many inspiring tasks prepared for me." Later he married his wife's younger sister.

One of the most absurd claims is that healing cannot be God's intentional Will because then no one would ever die. Surely fruits fall from the trees when they are ripe; they do not have to become wormy or diseased. Neither do humans have to be racked with pain or deformed by paralysis so that the world will not become over-populated. When a life has accomplished its purpose, the spirit can return to its Maker. We graduate from the schoolroom of this life into the Joy of the Lord in the Larger Life if we have so lived as to prepare for this next step.

Death is not the worst thing that can happen to a committed Christian although often the world seems to imply this in its attitudes. Death is release into the Perfect Presence of our Lord. To one who has found true spiritual healing, it holds no fear but rather reunion with loved ones who have gone on ahead into the Kingdom of Heaven. For those who are ill it is the *last* earthly healing, a release from the body's pain and disease as the human spirit leaves to rejoin its Maker. In an earlier statement to His disciples, Jesus said that He was going to prepare a place for them in His Father's house. In a Bible class a minister added, "If this place is good enough for Jesus, it is good enough for us!" To the thief repentant on the cross, Jesus said, "I tell you this: today you shall be with me in Paradise" (Luke 23:40-43). A body that had been nailed to a cross must have been healed in Paradise.

In such a discussion we must remember that although the healing of the mind and body is to be prayed for earnestly, the healing of the spirit is of primary concern. Our Lord dignified the human body by being made Man, and His resurrected Body was certainly not the mutilated, bloody one that was laid in the tomb on the first Good Friday! He was healed in the Resurrection of the suffering inflicted on Him by jealous, bigoted, cruel men. His sacrifice for the redemption of human sin enables man to be spiritually healed by the acceptance of His Love. I agree with Dr. Davey: "Health in the Christian understanding, is a continuous and victorious encounter with the powers that deny the existence and goodness of God. It is participation in an invasion of the realm of evil in which final victory lies beyond death, but the power of that victory is known now in the gift of the life-giving Spirit."[3]

Obedience

In the meantime we can go on in faith, knowing that our responsibility is to *obey* our Lord's commission to His Church through His Apostles "to proclaim the kingdom of God and to heal" the sick (Luke 9:1-6). Jesus gave the same commission to the seventy (the laity, one might say) as to the twelve and they also became His channels of healing of mind, body, spirit and soul. He promised us: "be assured, I am with you always, to the end of time" (Matthew 28:20).

We may not know all the answers, but we can pray in faith: "May the healing mercies of the risen Lord Jesus Christ, Who is present here with us now enter into your soul, your mind, your body, and heal you from all that harms you and give you His Peace." This prayer was used by the Rev. George Bennett during laying-on of hands at my first healing service in London. At that altar rail began the English chapter of the adventure with Christ which led to my desire to write this book: to share with fellowseekers at home and abroad my experiences and insights in the healing ministry of the Church on both sides of the Atlantic.

IV

JESUS THE HEALER

In my own search it was comforting and challenging to find that Divine Healing is firmly rooted in Holy Scripture—it is *not* a "new thought". Let us look in more detail at the Biblical record of Jesus not only as the Redeemer but also the Healer. He healed as part of His redemptive work of ushering in the Kingdom of God which He came to inaugurate. He acted out of His great compassion and desire that all men should have life and have it more abundantly. He healed as part of the doing of His Father's Will, part of the battle against Satan to whom He ascribed disease (Luke 13:16).

While living in England I came to know as a friend one of the foremost writers on this subject. In *Intelligent Prayer* the Rev. Lewis Maclachlan makes a strong statement that Jesus died as the Saviour not only to set us free from sin but also from disease. His prayers emphasized thanksgiving. Can we honestly say that the redeeming (healing of the soul) of Matthew the tax extortioner or of Mary Magdalene was of any more importance to Jesus than the setting free of the whole personality of the woman who had been paralyzed for eighteen long years? Was the cleansing of the lepers of that most dread and socially taboo disease any less redemptive because it included the healing of the body as well as the restoration of the outcast souls? Was the casting out of the demons from the mind, body and soul of the Gerasene man who had lived among the tombs a work of redemption or of healing or both?

Unfortunately I have found that the modern Church as a whole does not accept Jesus' concept of *total* redemption which He proclaimed not only in the preaching of His first sermon expounding the Scriptures *but also in the healing miracles* He performed. We can be thankful that more Churches are awakening from their lethargy of doubt, but they are still the exceptions. Bible study prayer groups help to uphold the ministry of healing by creating a climate of expectant faith.

How did Jesus authenticate His claim to Messiah-ship when John the Baptist sent a message from prison to know if He was the One? Jesus wanted John's messengers to see for themselves, rather than base their report on hearsay, so He delayed His answer until He had healed many blind people and other sufferers of various diseases, even evil spirit dominations. Then He said, "Go . . . and tell John what you have seen and heard: how the blind recover their sight, the lame walk, the lepers are clean, the deaf hear, the dead are raised to life, the poor are hearing the good news—and happy is the man who does not find me a stumbling-block" (Luke 7:22-23). Has the modern Church found Jesus the Healer a "stumbling block"?

Jesus began His earthly ministry by reading in the synagogue from Isaiah: "The spirit of the Lord is upon me because he has anointed me; He has sent me to announce good news to the poor, To proclaim release for prisoners and recovery of sight for the blind; To let the broken victims go free, To proclaim the year of the Lord's favour" (Luke 4:18, 19). He was in fact proclaiming the twin ministries of preaching and teaching with the healing of the sick—the authentic manifestation of the New Age, the Kingdom of God which He had come to bring on earth. Surely we cannot doubt the record which so clearly evidences the importance Jesus Himself placed on the healing ministry as part of His total proclamation of the Good News.

In Sweden, in my talks on healing prayer, we found it helpful to consider carefully the various ways Jesus healed and the conditions for healing. This book is an outcome of friends' requests to put these insights in writing.

(1) *By spoken word and touch in response to the faith of the patient.* To the leper who begged help, saying, "Sir, if only you will, you can cleanse me", Jesus replied, stretching out His hand to heal, "Indeed I will; be clean

again." Our Lord did not say, "It's better for you to learn patience"—He healed the man instantly! He did not say, "It's God's Will for you to suffer"—He demonstrated God's Will for healing. Jesus did not say, "God is more concerned with your soul than your body"—He replied, "Be clean again" (Matthew 8:1-4).

(2) *By the touching of the "hem of His garment" (unbeknown to our Lord in the crowd) even though the disease was of long standing.* To the woman who had faith to believe that she would thus be healed of hemorrhages suffered for twelve years, Jesus said kindly, "My daughter, your faith has cured you. Go in peace" (Luke 8:43-38). Also, in the cases of the woman paralyzed for eighteen years and the grown man who had been blind since birth, we see that it made no difference to Jesus how long the sufferer had been ill (Luke 13:10-17 and John 9:1-38). It did matter to the rulers of the synagogue that He healed on the sabbath day, breaking their man-made religious laws!

(3) *By removal of the block guilt, i.e., by the forgiveness of sin.* Jesus implied that in many cases disease is brought on the patient by his own personal sin, which is, in effect, the breaking of spiritual laws (John 5:1-15). To the crippled man by the pool of Bethesda who complained with guilt and self-pity, Jesus (after healing him) said, "Now that you are well again, leave your sinful ways, or you may suffer something worse."

(4) *By rebuking the disease.* In the case of Simon's mother-in-law, Jesus healed her instantly by rebuking the fever. And later he rebuked the devils in many persons among those brought to him to be cured (Luke 4:38-41).

(5) *By His great compassion.* When He saw the weeping widow whose only son had died, Jesus spoke with authority, "Young man, rise up!" and the dead man sat up and began to talk (Luke 7:11-17). Similarly, in compassion for Mary and Martha, the sisters bereaved by their brother's death, Jesus raised Lazarus from the dead (John 11:1-44).

(6) *By evoking expectancy and obedience in the sufferers.* The lepers were told to go and show themselves to the priests, and it must have taken a great deal of faith for them to start out, considering the current dread of leprosy. They

were not healed until *after* they had gone obediently on their way. Expecting healing and *acting as if they were healed,* they were made clean. However, only the one who returned to give thanks was made whole; he received the highest healing—whereas apparently the others got well only physically—because thanksgiving released in him the healing of spirit, soul and mind as well as of body (Luke 17:11-19).

(7) *By using outward signs.* Jesus led the blind man at Bethsaida out of the village, spat on his eyes and laid His hands on him for restoration of sight. At first the man was only partially healed. So he received a second laying-on of hands by Jesus, whereupon his sight was perfectly restored (Mark 8:22-26).

(8) *By using willingness (even when faith was weak) and His own deep prayers.* When the disciples had been unable to cast out the spirit causing epilepsy in a man's son, Jesus (because of the depth of His own prayer life) could use even the father's cry of "I have faith . . . help me where faith falls short" (Mark 9:14-29).

(9) *By using the faith of others than the sick.* In the case of the paralytic brought by the four friends who let him down through the tiled roof, Jesus saw their determination, their zeal and earnestness, their faith that at all costs the sick man must get to His feet. Our Lord used them as channels of healing when the patient was unable to walk, just as He uses today those who bring to Him through His Body the Church all who are too weak to come themselves. We bring them "on the stretchers of our prayers" or in person, expecting Jesus to heal them (Luke 5:17-26).

(10) *By using the faith of His disciples and casting out unbelievers.* Jesus took with Him to the bedside of Jairus's daughter only Peter, James and John (in addition to the parents) because He wanted to surround the young girl with a little prayer group. Thus He created a climate of faith in place of the lamenting, doubting atmosphere of the mourners. Then He took her hand and told her to get up. "Her spirit returned, she stood up immediately, and he told them to give her something to eat" (Luke 8:41, 42, 49-56).

(11) *By using the faith of others in spite of distance.* The centurion had great faith in the authority of Jesus because he

was himself a man of authority and he knew the power of the spoken word. But he also knew in his amazing humility that it must be the word of Jesus: that he himself was not worthy! Jesus used this foreigner's humble faith to channel His healing power by command even at a great distance—and "the messengers returned to the house and found the servant in good health" (Luke 7:2-10).

Could it be that we Christians today lack the humility, the faith, the obedience and the expectancy needed, that we hold back God's healing Will by our pride in man's superiority and human accomplishments? Do we too often doubt the efficacy of mere words of prayer? If the doctor says a disease is incurable, we are seldom able to say with the centurion, "Lord . . . I am not worthy to have you come under my roof . . . But say the word, and let my servant be healed" (Luke 7:2-10 RSV). Does the power of the word "cancer" overshadow the power of the name of Jesus, the Healer and Savior of the world?

Christ still stretches out His Hands to heal in mercy the weak, the weary and the heavy-laden: to re-integrate the distressed in mind, body, spirit and soul. May we who are called to be "His hands and His feet" bring to Him obediently in expectant faith those who are in need of His healing touch today! May His heart beat with our hearts, may His Holy Spirit intercede through our spirits so that the Grace of God can be bestowed today on human need as it was when He walked the dusty roads of Galilee! May the Church take up His promise: "In truth, in very truth I tell you, he who has faith in me will do what I am doing; and he will do greater things still because I am going to the Father" (John 14:12).

HEALING THROUGH DOCTORS

Religion and medicine need each other. As someone has said, "If we had to rely on our weak human faith alone, few of us would be alive today." We as Christians thank God for the wonders of medical science, for the dedication of doctors and nurses, especially when they have the humility to pray. Although they can prescribe and apply remedies, although they can cut away diseased tissues and graft in new ones, although they can set bones and apply casts—only God can heal!

Some psychiatrists realize that disturbed emotions (or "soul sickness") lie behind much of the so-called mental illness today. This in turn is too often reflected in the body because a human being is a living and interacting relationship of mind, body, spirit and soul. The psychiatrist can patiently trace the cause and effect of broken human relationships and unearth buried fears and resentments, but only God can forgive sin and release the depressed patient from the burden of guilt. Though drugs may temporarily relieve the patient's tension and dull his hypersensitiveness to worry, only God can give the Peace that passes understanding. *That* truly integrates human personality. "We need today the medicine of theology as well as the 'theology' of medicine", remarked the first critic of this manuscript.

In the first centuries after Christ, the Christian Churches were centers of healing where sufferers were brought to the apostles and those who followed after them in ministering Christ's healing power to the sick. One might say that the Churches were the first hospitals. Many fine hospitals today are still sponsored by Christian Churches, especially on mission fields.

It is a valid question then to ask why healing died out in the Church. When Christianity became the accepted religion after the Emperor Constantine was converted, it was actually weakened in point of faith by the inclusion of respectable, apathetic people who were baptized more because it became the fashionable thing to do rather than because of a deep conviction of repentance and saving faith in Jesus Christ. As faith grew weaker, so miracles of healing became less frequent; not that God had changed His mind, but rather because the faith of the Church had become watered down and there was less of a channel through which our Lord could work. Then, as medical science began to emerge, people began to look less to God and more to man. This shift was also true in the field of art which until the Renaissance era was a means of glorifying God but later began to glorify man. As Humanism crept into orthodox Christianity, faith in God became more of an intellectual exercise. Finally, the idea of a compartmentalized life took the place of the unified life, and man's body was treated as if it were an end in itself rather than as a totality, affected by mind, spirit and soul.

Nevertheless, the first doctors seen by many of the newer nations of the world were Christian missionary doctors and their first hospitals were usually supported by Christian Churches. Medical missions have helped to bridge the gap and heal the "divorce" between religion and medicine. The Church pioneered; and finally governments added their greater financial support. The key is the medical missionary, the Mission Hospital doctor, who lives out his faith in his practice. He represents his profession with competence; but he depends consciously on his God in practicing his ministry of medical mercy.

It is surely right that the Church and medicine work hand in hand. In addition to its direct ministry, the Church should support (by love, faith and prayer) the healing that comes from God through doctors, nurses and hospitals; they are His instruments and extensions of His healing touch, whether they are fully conscious of this or not.

For the most part, however, during the past hundred years when scientific medicine suddenly made great strides forward, there was the tendency in the world (lay as well as medical) to make a god out of science. People in the flush of this new learning forgot they were only discovering laws that were originated by the Great Creator.

In his article "Looking Forward", the former medical missionary, Dr. Michael Wilson, wrote: "Health means wholeness, completeness, and no man can be truly healthy apart from God. God made us for Himself, and if God is not in the center of our lives, we are seriously incomplete. This is the fundamental fact concerning our human nature."[1]

Reactionaries in the Church clung to outdated ideas of the Truth and antagonized those who were eagerly exploring the new fields that science was opening up for them in medicine. Instead of each side thanking God for the other (thus co-operating in His Will for healing) the Church for the most part insisted on the old idea that suffering was sent by God. As we have discussed, this was originally a Jewish concept denied in the earthly ministry of Christ but revived in the Medieval prayers for healing ("If it be Thy Will").

It was inevitable that serious conflict arose between religion (holding the position of thesis) and science (going to the other extreme of antithesis); but now, thanks be to God, we are entering an age of synthesis. The exuberance of science is becoming aware that in spite of the wonders achieved by man's intellect which is God-given, there is still a need for God to guide us in our use of these discoveries. To quote Dr. Wilson again: "The healing ministry of the Church will best be forwarded by the Christian penetration of scientific work. What God is building up through science must be brought under the acknowledged Kingship of Christ, and interpenetrated by all the Christian insights of prayer, fellowship, forgiveness and reconciliation. Curing diseases is but one part of the work of making persons whole."[2]

Fortunately, the reactionary and dogmatic attitude of the Church is giving way to a new realization of the importance of a close relationship between faith in God and medical science. We are now aware of the necessity to treat the *whole* man, who is not a disembodied spirit nor a body without a soul but a complete personality. His interacting body, mind, spirit and soul require the total healing coming from God through His joint channels, the Church and physicians. We need *both:* not either one alone!

In the past few years, more and more doctors and pastors have been realizing the need to co-operate to bring God's highest healing powers into the problems and tensions of modern life. Although medical science has won battles against most epidemic diseases which were the plagues of the past, the modern scourge of mental and emotional illnesses will require more than science alone can contribute. Harmony of the whole personality is the result of "God's loving action upon all and every part of our nature". The *Supplement of the British Medical Journal* of November 8, 1947, made a plea for co-operation between the Medical Association and the Churches' Council of Healing. Resentment, jealousy, fear, indulgence and carelessness were identified as destructive attitudes that impair the patient's health and retard his recovery.

In one great clinic in America it has been reported that three quarters of the patients are treated for non-organic illnesses; and functional illnesses if prolonged indefinitely can become organic. The emotional conflicts (if not resolved) are often repressed until they erupt as mental illnesses, if not physical. Of course not all illness is so obviously a result of dangerous emotions as are ulcers, for example; but the doctor's advice not to worry is more difficult to follow than any medical prescription! It is a spiritual prescription and can be filled only as the patient finds a faith for living.

Although psychosomatic medicine can tell us what disorders will most likely be created by the unhealthy emotions of fear, resentment or guilt, it cannot give us the transforming Power needed to overcome these attitudes. This is the contribution of religion. Serums, pills, X-ray treatments and operations can alleviate, diagnose or repair damage but they do not offer immunity against future outbreaks because they treat only the *results or symptoms,* not the *causes* of a great percentage of our modern illnesses. Diabetes, heart trouble, high blood pressure, rheumatoid arthritis, asthma, skin diseases, and even the common cold are felt by many reputable doctors (if not by the medical profession as a whole) to be to a great extent emotionally caused over a of time. According to the late Dr. Griffith Evans, the Medical

Research Council in England has conducted experiments for twenty-five years hoping to determine whether people's emotions help to make them more immune to the common cold. In situations where love and joy prevail, this seemed to make an important difference.

Despondency and anger are recognized by many doctors as emotions that trip the balance and condition us to susceptibility to many diseases. Dr. Evans wrote in his study, *Cancer:* "[man's] immune reaction defends him from malignant growth as well as from infection. . . . It takes two years for the normal cells to be degraded by the slow 'weak' neutrinal or psychic reaction to wear down their inherent resistance (also known as the 'energy resonance'). So long as the cells are only 'initiated', a state in which they still are subject to the governing laws of the body, the cancerous inclination is reversible. The process is general whether the inclination is to cancer, or to degeneration or to a recognizable psychosomatic disorder. The remedy, therefore, also is general—all physical treatment should be subordinate to the restoration of spiritual (not merely mental) well-being."[3]

In analyzing case histories of cancer patients, Dr. Evans added: "All exhibited *secret* sorrows, troubles which could not be discussed even with the closest friends. The distress situation is always an internal one. This experience led me to look directly for a mental stress factor in all cases of cancer seen. Such a factor was present in just over half of all cases."[4]

Could this be the reason why research has not been able to identify conclusively a cancer virus or other medically detectable cause? "Mental stress" does not show on an X-ray or in a test-tube, and in most cases it cannot be willed away. Peace of mind cannot be bought in a bottle or injected by a hypodermic, but it can come from God as the patient lives by faith in His Power to sustain and to bring good out of any situation that is truly entrusted to Him. "Secret sorrows" can be touched by the deep penetration of the patient's realization of God's unconditional Love; and His forgiveness of sin can wipe out guilts that cannot be discussed with close friends. This is not to imply that all sickness is a result of personal sin. In America, the Medical Societies of most states have committees co-operating with clergy in treating the whole man.

We can be thankful that more and more doctors on both sides of the Atlantic are standing out as leaders in the field of Christian medical practice, often overtaxing themselves to bring this broader understanding of healing, not only to lay people who are their patients, but also to their medical colleagues. One might even think of these consecrated doctors as pioneers, like Pasteur and Lister, for they are pioneering in the field of "Medicine and Religion". Dr. Paul Tournier, the eminent Swiss doctor, in *A Doctor's Casebook in the Light of the Bible,* suggests that spiritual power may cause a more rapid healing than would have been expected under the usual biological conditions. He quotes Le Compte du Nouy as saying that chemical responses and cicatrization operate under the same laws. As a Christian, Dr. Tournier succeeds in relating his faith to his practice of medicine in a most helpful way.

One of America's outstanding specialists in the field of rheumatoid arthritis, Dr. Loring T. Swaim, conducted a twenty-five-year-long study of his arthritic patients from whom he got complete "medical", "relationship", and "spiritual" case histories. He found that unhappy emotional pressures (usually of long duration) were the forerunners of arthritic problems and that fresh outbreaks were apt to follow renewed bitterness, especially where close relatives were involved. He reports that as he and the patients worked together in a Christian attitude of listening prayer to God, the healing results were amazing. With the doctor's help, the patients came to find that their Heavenly Father was concerned with them as individuals. They exchanged their self-concern for a deep and abiding faith which apparently had been a missing influence, often because resentments had separated them from God as well as from other human beings. Ultimately, for many patients, their new experience of God's Love became more significant than their illnesses. In reading Dr. Swaim's book, many have found their faith strengthened and their arthritis receding. His contagious faith is a real spiritual tonic for any sick person.

We can also rejoice when a physicist such as the late Dr.

Samuel Williams of Amherst College speaks of God's transforming power as something that can be accepted with the same confidence of validity as laboratory experiments. The results of the tests he had witnessed were significantly changed lives.

A fine general practitioner spends time in prayer with his patients as well as in his own daily personal devotions. He urges his medical colleagues as well as his patients to look for a reality of Christ in their daily lives. For several years as a dedicated layman he has been helping others to find the salvation of their spirits for eternity as well as the healing of their bodies in his God-given ministry of medicine.

Although the insights and conclusions of these Christian doctors have inspired the writing of this chapter, there are still others too numerous to mention. May God's grace sustain and guide them, using them to open the hearts and minds of all they contact to the awareness of God's purposes for total healing. May they continue with urgency to explore the workings of the spiritual laws of the universe, remembering that the whole personality (spirit, soul, mind and body) must be harmonized with God's eternal purposes through His Holy Spirit. For the true being to emerge, we must live in acceptance of ourselves and with all of God's laws through union with Himself. God created us for fellowship with Himself, and He will never rest until we have become reintegrated through spiritual rebirth into the new life which is our true nature, beginning now but reaching into all eternity. It is indeed of interest that the following challenge should come from Dr. Wilson (who, as we have seen, is both a medical doctor and a clergyman): "We recall our churches to see the healing task as implicit in our Lord's commission to His disciples."[5]

We thank God for men who patiently spend their lives in research to develop new medical methods of healing; and for an increasing number of doctors who acknowledge that they are merely instruments of His healing power for their patients' bodies. We thank God for hospitals today that admit humbly, "We dress the wounds, God heals." We thank God for praying Christians who unite their intercessions for doctors, nurses, pastors and all who minister to the sick in every level of personality.

HEALING THROUGH INTERCESSORS

It was many years after my initial healing experience before I was asked to join my first prayer group. Through these new friends I learned that the members of a prayer group are acting in accordance with an ancient and scriptural custom and a valid promise of our Lord Himself when they meet together to pray for someone in need of healing and wholeness. They meet not just in compassion and faith but in obedience to Him. They stand upon our Lord's promises recorded in St. Matthew's Gospel: "Again I tell you this: if two of you agree on earth about any request you have to make, that request will be granted by my heavenly Father. For where two or three have met together in my name, I am there among them" (19:19,20). We recalled St. James' oft-quoted Epistle: "Is one of you ill? He should send for the elders of the congregation to pray over him and anoint him with oil in the name of the Lord. The prayer offered in faith will save the sick man, the Lord will raise him from his bed, and any sins he may have committed will be forgiven" (5:14, 15).

Sometimes the "two in agreement" are two mothers drawn together by a mutual concern for the child of one of them. After our son's miraculous healing of asthma in the middle of the night while I knelt in prayer beside his bed, it seemed that God often laid it on my heart to pray for others, especially children. But not for many years was the courage given me to go and pray audibly for a sick person. In 1947, the faith of the Church was much weaker than it is today. I had tried to discuss my own experience of "amazing grace" with various clergy in different cities where we had lived but their scepticism tended to weaken my faith. So I decided just to pray silently without telling anyone.

Eventually, it became evident that God was honoring even these prayers, for His healing touch was manifested in amazing recoveries of several people: a child critically ill of spinal meningitis, a fine young father who was expected to die of polio, and later his wife who had a very serious heart attack. Of course there were undoubtedly many others praying; the doctors were mystified, but I was not! These experiences strengthened my faith "to go, nothing doubting" when a desperate friend telephoned, begging me to come and pray for the healing of her baby's ear trouble. As the piercing screams came through the telephone, there seemed no other answer. Her doctor was out of town and obviously this anguished mother had faith that God could use me even if I did not feel myself an adequate channel. Knowing that God loved her little child as much as He loved mine, I suddenly realized that it did not depend on me anyway. Here was this young mother's faith; so all that was required of me was to be obedient to the insistent urge within me that would not seem to take "No" for an answer!

The two of us were in agreement that it was not God's Will for this poor baby to suffer, so we just prayed that Jesus would touch her through our hands as we laid them gently over the sore ear. The baby stopped crying and soon fell asleep. We continued to lift her to God in prayers of thanksgiving throughout the day as we two mothers went about our household duties. When the doctor returned to town the next day, he checked the child's ears and could scarcely believe she had had such pain. Two years later, she had had no recurrences of ear trouble, much to her mother's surprise and joy. God's mercy is limitless if we trust in *Him*, not in ourselves.

How wonderful if we could always accept healing as little children usually do. The three-year-old granddaughter of a friend was suffering from an asthmatic attack when I was asked to drop in to have a prayer with her. As the little girl lay listlessly on the sofa, her mother, grandmother and great-grandmother drew their chairs closer. We talked to Rena about Jesus—who loved her enough to touch her through my hands as I prayed a simple prayer of faith.

Months later in another city when she was visiting her aunt who had a severe headache, Rena insisted on her telephoning me long distance to pray for the headache, saying, "She will ask Jesus to make me well and He will. She prayed and asked Jesus to make me well, and He did." No wonder that it is often easier to pray for a child than for an adult.

Sometimes the "two in agreement" are a mother and child, for Jesus warned: "the kingdom of God belongs to such as these. I tell you, whoever does not accept the kingdom of God like a child will never enter it" (Mark 10:14, 15). Little children have a more trusting faith that seems to become tarnished as they grow into the age of self-dependence. Having prayed, they leave the matter in God's hands, whereas their elders too often hamper God's plans by trying to take the problem back to work it out according to their own blueprints. Glenn Clark told at a CFO retreat of a boy who interrupted his game to pray for his mother when she was suffering from a sick headache. Immediately after he had ended his rather brief prayer, the boy returned hurriedly to the game. When she thought of remonstrating with him for his seeming lack of concern, the mother realized that nonetheless the headache had gone! Later she queried her son who replied: "Why should I wait around? After all, I turned it over to God and it was up to Him to heal you!" No wonder the Bible says: "A little child shall lead them" (Isaiah 11:6 AV).

Many times, the "two in agreement" are a loving Christian couple, grateful for God's blessing of their lives, eager to be used as His channel of grace to others. One might hope also that it could be two school teachers praying for a difficult child who needs to be made whole by the Love of God flowing through the prayers of the faithful. A world-renowned missionary has said that a congregation can be changed in its attitudes if two members offer themselves to be God's channels of Love (without judgment) to draw the Church into unity with Himself and with each other. A pastor and a worried parent can be the "two in agreement" praying for a delinquent young person. "Two in agreement", linked together over the telephone, can lift up a need in prayer so vital that it seems as if Christ Himself is standing between them and the miles no longer exist. A doctor and a nurse praying together before an especially difficult operation can be better channels for God's healing of their patient. Jesus and the centurion were in agreement about the servant's need. St. Matthew's Gospel records: "At that moment the boy recovered" (8:13).

In my earlier days as an intercessor, I went to a healing service to take the laying-on of hands as proxy for a friend named Harriett because as I approached the altar my guidance to do so was very strong. As the priest heard me whisper her name, he prayed the prayer of faith for God's healing touch to flow out to meet her needs. We were the "two in agreement" that this was God's Will. Later in the day Harriett reported that at the very same hour, although she had been expecting to go to the hospital for an operation, she was healed! At that moment she was upholstering a chair instead. In a matter of weeks Harriett also experienced a very deep and wonderful spiritual healing that brought her into the Church in the next confirmation class. She has since become an even greater channel of blessing to others for she *knows* personally the healing Love of God. Before this, it had been difficult for her as a nursing supervisor to accept the fact that Jesus is capable of healing in ways beyond scientific understanding. Jesus healed through the faith of some of His channels (such as the centurion who came on behalf of his servant). Today, in our "watered-down, do-it-yourself Christianity" we are often unaware that Jesus still heals. We can be thankful for psychosomatic medicine which discovered as a science that the causative factors in most illnesses are non-physical (emotional), even though the pain itself is very real.

The resevoir of God's Love is great enough to meet any need, but there must often be a pipe-line of faith through whom this Divine Love can be released. Water in a huge resevoir cannot reach a withering plant unless the gardener connects a hose and turns on the tap. All he has to do is to make the connection: if it is a leaky one, much of the water will be wasted; and if the hose does not reach the plant, it will not be saved, no matter how full the resevoir. The gardener exercises faith as he points the hose in the right direction. He does not revive the plant, nor does he have to carry the water, but he does have to make the proper connection and release the valve. Likewise, the intercessor does not revive or heal the patient. He merely acts in faith as the hose (or pipe-line) that connects the one in need with the Divine Source of Love so that rivers of Living Water can restore the soul that is hungering and thirsting after righteousness.

The cleaner the pipe-line, the clearer the water. Therefore, when we are asking God to use us as His channel of healing for others, it is also important to ask Him to purify our own hearts. "Create in me a right spirit, O Lord," should be our first prayer. A friend once prayed: "Remove from me the rust of resentments and long-harbored grudges, the sticks of pride, the rocks of self-will, O God, that I may become a clearer channel for the outflowing of Thy Grace and Healing Power." Jesus said, "If you dwell in me, and my words dwell in you, ask what you will, and you shall have it" (John 15:7).

How dare we pretend to be *dwelling in Christ,* if we are *dwelling upon* past hurts and injuries to our pride? Do we care more about our status with others than His status in us? True, we can never earn His grace, but we can most effectively thwart it! Can we in all conscience ask in His Name, when we are harbouring an attitude of mind and heart that is contrary to His Nature of Love? How much we need His humility, His trustful dependence on our Father, His compassionate Love!

An elderly lady suffering from a spastic colon and a fearful, anxious spirit once asked me to pray for her to be lifted from the depression which was obviously a major part of her physical trouble. Time and again this distressed lady received wonderful help from God and was relieved of mental and physical anguish. It was not necessary to visit her, nor did the doctor have to prescribe new medicine. As intercessor, I had only to relax in the Peace of God and ask for His Peace to flow through me into this friend in need. It was not necessary to be a trained psychiatrist but only to call upon the Holy Spirit to lead us both into His Truth. He alone could give the thoughts needed for deep healing of the patient's subconscious mind which was still grieving over buried remorse and guilt, much of it unwarranted. To the old lady's amazement, gradually all the hurts and distressing memories dissolved as the Love and Light of Christ were channelled to shine into those deep recesses of her subconscious which still retained the bitterness of the past. In a climate of prayer, the Holy Spirit was able to guide her to such an open and humble attitude of mind that she could sort out the true guilts from the imagined (or false ones) and be healed by Christ's forgiving Love. She suddenly realized that our Lord through His Holy Spirit was teaching her to release these problems of life to Him in a relationship of perfect trust and love—and even joy! As we shall see in a later chapter, emotions when held long enough can become fixed spirits of fear, anxiety, resentment, despair and so forth. When they have been pushed down too long in our subconscious minds, they begin to possess us.

Jesus said, "I am the vine, and you the branches. He who dwells in me, as I dwell in him, bears much fruit; for apart from me you can do nothing" (John 15:5). As intercessors, are we not merely branches of the one true Vine? The branch does not produce the fruit; it is the sap, or the Life within, that makes the fruit grow. It is not the intercessor's wisdom or human love but the divine Wisdom and Love of the indwelling and abiding Christ who creates the healing. Listen to His words: "I am not myself the source of the words I speak to you: it is the Father who dwells in me doing his own work. Believe me when I say that I am in the Father and the Father in me; or else accept the evidence of the deeds themselves. In truth, in very truth I tell you, he who has faith in me will do what I am doing; and he will do greater things still because I am going to the Father. Indeed anything you ask in my name I will do, so that the Father may be glorified in the Son. If you ask anything in my name I will do it" (John 14:10-14).

A group of some twenty earnest members of our parish Church listened to a tape recording of a challenging talk after the end of an inspiring four-day mission on Divine Healing. All of us present felt singularly full of faith in God's Will to heal. Someone asked that in prayer we lift into the Healing Presence of the Lord an elderly member of the choir. Aileen had been critically ill and was at that moment in a coma. We asked the Holy Spirit to intercede through us as the "two or three" mentioned by our Lord. In one accord we visualized Jesus touching Aileen with His healing Power as she lay in her hospital room. There was great Peace, a sense of the fulfilment of the promise "I am there among them". And in confident trust we went home at eight-thirty, leaving her in His care. The next day Aileen's son telephoned our rector to say that to the amazement of all, his mother had come out of the coma the evening before at exactly eight-thirty and was feeling greatly improved. Some weeks later Aileen's dearest wish was fulfilled; she sang in the choir at the Easter Choral Communion, praising God for His healing power today.

When my first book was published, a newspaper printed a picture of my rector and me at the "Autograph Tea" being given by my parish. A woman called Nancy telephoned me because she had read the article and felt impelled to make this first faltering step of faith. She was the daughter of a devout Methodist minister and had led a very busy life full of good works but not much real prayer. At the age of fifty-five she had suffered a serious heart attack and had become very discouraged when her doctor finally told her, "You might as well reconcile yourself to being a semi-invalid for the rest of your life." One morning in desperation, she threw herself on God's mercy. A few minutes later as she picked up the newspaper her attention was focused on this picture and she felt that she needed to read my book. Through a fantastic series of "God-incidences" (not "coincidences"), in a few hours I was able to go to pray with her, leaving her the book.

Within a few weeks we moved to a new home in her neighborhood, and she began to go with me to a large interdenominational prayer group which I was then leading. Nancy and I believed that God had guided me into her life for this purpose. Her first impression of the prayer group was that we were certainly well-meaning, kind women, so she silently prayed during our meeting: "O God, I can't believe the way they do, but please don't let my lack of faith hold back what You are doing through their prayers." Within a few weeks she had become a regular member. During a routine appointment with her doctor he looked at her in a very startled way and asked what she had been doing. When she told him, he seemed pleased. Her heart condition improved steadily until the doctor finally released her from his care. She was free to lead a perfectly normal life and even began to learn to drive her car.

When I moved away she became the leader of this prayer group where she had first prayed that her own lack of faith would not interfere with God's healing power! Her doctor often told other patients to telephone Nancy because he noticed that her contagious faith helped to allay their fears. I thank God for giving me a dear friend and most faithful prayer partner. A desperate telephone call from a stranger can be part of a healing adventure with Christ.

In intercessory prayer those who have faith in the healing Christ offer themselves humbly to be God's channels through whom His power flows out to many in need. All of us are constantly transmitting our thoughts and emotions to others, so it behooves us to be sure that they are healing ones. It is best that the patient be aware of the prayers and "in tune", either by being physically present or by thinking of the group at the appointed time even when physically absent. But experience has proved that thousands of people have been helped by God's action through prayers of "faithful believers" when the sick person was not aware of this activity. And, even when a sceptic might scoff if he knew, God has often used the earnest prayers of those who have come to the Throne of Grace on his behalf. The faith of a group intertwined in compassion can be used to lift the sick one to Jesus on the "stretcher of prayer". We are like the four friends in the Bible who brought the paralyzed man, lowering him through the roof on a pallet or stretcher so that Jesus could heal him.

Often I am asked, "How do you start a prayer group?" There are as many ways as there are groups, for each one is "born" (not organized) out of need. When two or three people become aware of their need to share their faith and love in prayer to God for themselves, their families, their Church, their neighbours, their country and the world, a prayer group is born. Some begin over a cup of coffee when a neighbor blurts out a desperate need and finds God's help through the prayer of her compassionate friend; and as each one is blessed in the sharing, more neighbors are drawn into this fellowship of understanding love and prayer, meeting informally in a home at the same time each week. Others are born out of a Church Lenten Study program when at the end of the six weeks a nucleus of those attending feel their fellowship of study and prayer is too meaningful to drop. Others follow naturally after a Church's healing mission, Lay Witness mission, Faith-at-Work mission, or Renewal mission. The pastor usually invites all interested persons to a meeting where such groups emerge spontaneously as a part of his Church's weekly fare for those who are hungry enough spiritually to set aside time for regular meeting. Often these are Bible Study prayer groups. But there are many good thought-provoking, challenging books and tape recordings that lead to deeper commitment and a better understanding of prayer. A prayer group is not a debating club. It is a sharing fellowship of those who care about the Lord and each other enough to dare to lift any need to Him in prayer. Numbers are not important; but love and unity of spirit grow as the prayer group lets the Lord lead them into His purpose, drawing to them other like-minded persons. The private devotional life of each member is part of its strength.

Of course the Holy Spirit is the real Leader through whomever He finds usable, open to His leading. It is an appointment with God taking precedence over any other, such as a hairdresser's appointment. My own preference is for a meeting (one or one and one-half hours weekly) which opens with prayer for the leading of the Holy Spirit; centers around twenty to thirty minutes of study, leading into a "circle of prayer"; then ends with witnessing to the glory of God. Each person should feel free to talk to God aloud in prayer without fear of criticism or gossiping. For those afraid to pray aloud, a silent prayer is just as valid and a spoken "Amen" ("So be it") enables the next person to take her turn. The group should be Jesus-centered enough to give the problems and needs to Him who alone can answer them.

Not all prayer groups meet together in person. Sometimes the Lord creates a oneness of spirit across even vast distances—by means of prayer manuals or healing magazines that unite intercessors through their articles, daily Bible meditations and prayers. Some use monthly intercession lists sent out by an "area secretary". Members join in spirit daily, preferably at a regular time, lifting up the whole widespread intercession work. Requests for prayer (as they come in by mail or telephone) are prayed for by the central group in a specific service, but the undergirding by the individual and scattered intercessors is an important part of the whole work. Names placed in a Prayer Box or Book of Healing are prayed for as a group, knowing that as Christ healed the multitudes, so He can touch each of the lives thus offered to Him. Petitioners sending in requests and intercessors are God's channels to those in need.

At a healing service names read aloud at the altar are those who need to receive God's blessing upon their lives; for the sake of privacy only given names are customarily used. It is generally better not to recite details of each illness or need although names may be grouped in certain categories (physical, marital, guidance, conversion and the like). The Rev. Edward Winckley once said, "God does not need an 'organ recital' "—and we might add that even the faith of the staunchest believer wanes when a lengthy list of critical illnesses is intoned! In His Omniscience, we can trust God to know which "Mary" is being offered to His loving care, since He is the God "to whom all hearts are open, all desires known, and from whom no secrets are hid." To avoid repetition an initial may be added to the Christian name. To me, nicknames such as "Tubby" or "Snookie" seem hardly proper at the altar in a healing service when the baptismal name seems more appropriate because it has more spiritual meaning.

True intercession is bringing the patient into a closer relationship with God the Healer. His willingness to heal is often blocked because our human capacity to receive limits the effectiveness of His divine Love. When the sick one is supported by the love and faith of a community of believers interceding for him, a barrier to healing is removed and the flow of God's healing power is released. Jesus cast out unbelievers when He healed Jairus's daughter. Can we not imagine His feeling about the unbelief which characterizes most Churches today? Let us use our imaginations constructively so that we "see" the person *whole* as God created him to be, not fixing our gaze on the latest negative medical report as a finality. Literally, many Christians are making plans to bury the sick one even before he has died. This is hardly the attitude of the Christ we purpose to follow, for He even raised the dead on three occasions. The faith of St. Paul was used to restore Eutychus to life!

Our best prayers are those which Christ prays in and through us for the purposes which He wills us to ask. In Florida our present parish Church is truly a center of spiritual healing for all who come in humility to find the Love of Jesus. Is it any wonder that people (lay and clergy) travel miles to mingle with those of many denominations at its altar? We thank God for ministers who have the faith to believe in the Risen Jesus as Healer and the humility to accept the ministry of the laity as our Lord uses the faith of intercessors of many denominations.

In my prayer-counselling ministry I have found that the energies of Divine Love have succeeded in many cases where shock treatments fail. It has also been obvious that where a praying, witnessing Church created a climate of faith, the spiritual energies released by God through His channels resulted in such healings as those of bursitis, fever, various pains and cripplings, diabetes, high blood pressure and cancer—to name a few. The pity is that so few modern Churches qualify as centers of praying and witnessing faith!

HEALING THROUGH MEANS OF GRACE

In services of His Church, through means of grace offered by our Lord we can find *wholeness,* which is much more than just getting well physically. It may require a "spiritual operation" of a special anointing or a laying-on of hands in a service of healing before the real cure can take place. It may be more important to restore a broken relationship than to set the person free from mental or physical pain. If there is something troubling the conscience of the patient, or some problem of relationships, the minister will know best how to call upon Divine Forgiveness and Healing Love to set the person free from emotional bondage. In time of serious illness, the pastor or priest should be asked to minister to the person's soul and spirit along with the doctor who treats the mind and body. The supplementing of each other's work under the guidance of the Holy Spirit results in more rapid, complete and lasting healing. Certainly it is ridiculous to wait until the patient has given up (or been given up) before calling the minister, the "spiritual doctor".

The British Medical Journal has stated that no tissue of the body is entirely free from the influence of the spirit. Divine Healing flows through the channels (individual, prayer group, or in the services of the Church) to stimulate natural recuperative powers and remove hindrances to healing. It is not too much to say that God's Will to heal is waiting for a proper channel to be provided; and that, without this, the divine energy might be blocked out of a patient's mind, body, spirit and soul. Prayer is co-operating with God and with the doctor as well, not competing with him but rather completing his work. As God's Love penetrates the spirit it stimulates the subconscious mind, and, through its influence, the body's powers to heal. God's Love moves the intellect or conscious mind in the direction of faith and hope. Therefore, the services of the Church as a means of grace should no more be neglected than the doctor's knowledge and skill.

Laying-On of Hands

The late Archbishop of Canterbury, William Temple, once wrote that the Christian doctor has recognized as his greatest ally "the unseen factor of spiritual regeneration". As we consider the following cases of healing, may we remember that this is not magic but the interpenetration of cells by the higher influence of the Spirit of God using the channels of faith that are offered to Him.

Elizabeth had been a semi-invalid after two unsuccessful heart operations, until she had a real encounter with the Living Lord after which she gradually received a very wonderful healing of her heart condition. The healing services of our Church had been used by God as one of His channels for healing Power to flow into her life. Whereas at first she had come for herself, now she came each week to take the laying-on of hands as "proxy" for someone else in need. She brought others with her and spent much time visiting sick people and counselling them over the telephone. But during an unusually busy Lenten season these Church meetings seemed doubled and family responsiblities suddenly increased. Elizabeth realized that an ominous pain had returned, a warning of the old symptoms she remembered only too well. Although her own heart was beating at a terrifying rate and the ache was almost unbearable, she whispered the name of a friend in urgent need. As the priest laid his hands on her head and prayed for the friend's healing, a wonderful sense of peace flooded Elizabeth's whole being. Thankful that she had received an instantaneous healing, she arose from her knees. It was a double blessing as the friend (whose own faith had not been great enough to come to the service for herself) was also gradually healed. The Lord has been continuously lifted up in Elizabeth's consecrated life.

The most important result of Divine Healing is personal commitment to Jesus. In *Christian Healing,* Dr. Evelyn Frost summarizes what we mean by healing as it relates to deeper commitment: "Thus the road to health is the road of sacrifice; in the pouring out of life the individual finds life, and in finding becomes both filled with the eternal life which is his own surest healing and also overflowing with such life, and thus a channel of healing for his environment."[1] In actual practice we see that only as one becomes a "channel of healing for his environment" is he really made *whole*, for the "overflowing" or sharing in some small way with others in need of the Love of Jesus seems *to complete his own healing.*

A woman in her late thirties went to her doctor because of the appearance of a suspicious lump. After careful examination he sent Helen to a surgeon for further diagnosis. To her dismay he confirmed the need for an operation to remove the tumor. Quietly the day before the operation Helen went in faith to a healing service of our church. All of us noticed a very real sense of Christ's Presence as together we knelt at the altar rail. There was a deepening awareness of His Peace as the vicar laid his hands on her head in prayer. When Helen went to the hospital, her surgeon could find no lump! He reviewed her record and checked again with the original diagnostician who confirmed the earlier diagnosis. Several years later, Helen, who had never had to have the operation, continued to be a channel of God's blessing to others in gratitude for what His merciful Love meant in her life.

The Rev. J. Cameron Peddie has been used by the Lord in Scotland for remarkable healings through the laying-on of hands. In his book, *The Forgotten Talent,* there is a splendid preface by A. D. Moffat (a prominent Glasgow pathologist) who recounts that Mr. Peddie's healing ministrations have often amazed physicians with whom he co-operates. Frequently there has been a quickened recovery in response to his prayers and sometimes healings in cases that were medically diagnosed as terminal. The ministry of this humble man of God began long ago when he formed the habit of silent communion at each midnight vigil. With Dr. Moffat we can hope that more ministers will be consecrated to such a ministry of healing as part of the Church's purpose in a sick world.

In the *Prayer Book Studies* published by the Standing Liturgical Commission of the Protestant Episcopal Church in

America, we find an explanation of this means of grace. "Throughout the period of the undivided Church, healing was taken for granted as a function of the ministry. Churches were considered 'temples of healing', and people resorted to them as we now go to hospitals. If a person was too sick to go to Church, the Bishop or Priest, accompanied by laymen of the congregation, visited him, and administered Holy Unction together with the Laying-on of Hands."[2]

Holy Unction

St. Mark's Gospel records that the disciples went forth at our Lord's express command "and many sick people they anointed with oil and cured" (6:13). By the time that St. James wrote his Epistle, the practice of anointing the sick with oil was quite well established.

While I was living in England (where my husband was stationed for over three years) my almost ninety-year-old mother found that the pressures of living alone in America had become too great, especially when she lost her sight. Her hearing had been miraculously restored but it was a very mixed blessing, for many noises which she had never noticed became most disturbing. She had been carrying a burden of prayer requests that would have daunted many younger persons, and because of her great compassion, she had slipped into the mistake of straining to help God answer them. Without realizing it, in her desire to be broadminded she had let go of the saving Power of Jesus Christ and had allowed herself to be drawn into a healing cult that omits the Atonement as central to its faith. A sudden shock precipitated a nervous breakdown which at first was thought to be hopeless senility. She was unable to see, unable to sleep and unable to pray.

When I flew home and saw her deep despair I knew why the Lord had given me the inner pressure of the words, "Go *now,* before it is too late!" In a Christian nursing home relieved of all tensions and "spiritually immersed" in prayers of love and faith, my mother's hope began to be restored. One by one, she turned over to God the persons whose prayer problems she had been trying unsuccessfully to solve. She asked me to teach her how to pray—holding on to Jesus in times of depression as "to Thy Cross I cling". Old gospel hymns and prayerful dependence upon the saving Grace of Jesus Christ again replaced the "do-it-yourself", tangent type of religion into which she had inadvertently slipped. Many times when in pain she would ask me to lay my hands on her head and pray for God's healing of Peace in her disturbed mind and emotions—and the tension would be relieved. Her doubts and fears were being dispelled as the Lord used the prayers of friends as transmitters of His Healing Light and Love. She learned to hold in her mind the same thoughts which I had been guided to use in contemplative meditation for her: "In quietness and confidence shall be my strength, in returning and rest I shall be saved"; and "Be still, and know that I am God, and take hold of My Peace within you."

When the young curate came to her room to anoint her for healing after a short service of Holy Communion, he prayed aloud the words: "I anoint thee with oil in the Name of the Father, and of the Son, and of the Holy Ghost; beseeching the mercy of our Lord Jesus Christ, that all thy pain and sickness of body being put to flight, the blessing of health may be restored unto thee."[3] At that very moment, kneeling close beside her, I "knew" within my heart these words: "She shall be healed that God may be glorified." Exhausted, my mother lay back on her pillow, almost as if she were too tired to live.

Two hours later she called for her Bible and said, "My eyes seem suddenly so much better. I think I can read." Joyously we opened to James 5:14-16 and she read aloud slowly but thankfully: "Is one of you ill? He should send for the elders of the congregation to pray over him and anoint him with oil in the name of the Lord. The prayer offered in faith will save the sick man, the Lord will raise him from his bed, and any sins he may have committed will be forgiven. Therefore confess your sins to one another, and pray for one another, and then you will be healed."

Our Healing Lord had touched her through the Church (priest and laywoman united in faith and obedient trust) to His glory, restoring her sight so that she could read her Bible and Prayer Book. From then on, she began to sing and smile again, almost like her former cheerful self. In great thanksgiving we continued to praise God who raises up His servants and blesses them through human channels of His Love. The purpose of Holy Unction as a sacramental act of healing is to assist the whole personality to surrender more fully to the Lord of Life, not just to seek the alleviation of pain. It is not the Anglican Church's last rites for the dying but for wholeness of life, ultimately stretching into eternity but beginning in this life.

Sacramental Confession

When one is unable to love one's "brother", one is not truly able to love God. I John 4:20 reminds us: "But if a man says, 'I love God', while hating his brother, he is a liar. If he does not love the brother whom he has seen, it cannot be that he loves God whom he has not seen." Indeed Christ commands that whoever loves God must also love his brother. A person must seek forgiveness from God if he holds bitterness against another person, no matter what the cause; and he must seek this, *not just because he wants to be freed from illness, physical or mental, but because of his greater desire for a right relationship with his God.*

Dr. Paul Tournier, the eminent Swiss doctor, lecturer and author, has pointed out the need for confession to be practised more freely in the Protestant Churches on both sides of the Atlantic. In a lecture at a Presbyterian seminary he reminded us that both Calvin and Luther believed in confession. Dr. Tournier has concluded from his medical practice that the need is great for people to hear, "God forgives you *personally.*" He spoke of a pastor to whom he (as a doctor) had to say those words, and yet this minister had preached on the grace of God hundreds of times without accepting God's forgiveness for himself! Dr. Tournier added: "Instead of trying to edify the Christian life so as to stand in no need of grace, we need to realize that sanctification comes by realizing our sins and confessing them to God."

Most churches encourage daily private confession of one's sins to God, as well as public or "general confession". But, realizing the need in many cases for persons to make their confession to God in the presence of a trained and ordained minister or priest, the Anglican Church provides Holy Penance or sacramental confession as an optional means of grace. Some persons carry such a deep sense of guilt that they seem not to be able to "accept" God's words of forgiveness unless they are spoken through a human being. Although in such a case a spiritual friend can often help in preparing the way for sacramental confession to take place, the authority of the Church through the minister seems to carry greater weight in the disturbed consciousness of one who has so long harbored a guilt complex that he cannot accept God's forgiveness and forgive himself. Our Lord said to His disciples, "If you forgive any man's sins, they stand forgiven; if you pronounce them unforgiven, unforgiven they remain" (John 20:23). It is believed that God's ordained ministers have this function, so these same words are used today in the Anglican ordination service. We must always be aware that our Lord began His earthly ministry by proclaiming: "Repent; for the kingdom of Heaven is upon you" (Matthew 4:17). True penitence precedes true healing of the whole person. The following experiences illustrate this point.

Jane, a woman with two young daughters, was separated from her husband and attributed most of the blame to her mother-in-law who seemed to delight in causing a severe rift between them. The bitterness of Jane's feelings was the root of a prolonged depression. It warped her whole attitude toward life. She had started coming to our church's prayer group at our rector's suggestion. Although she felt temporary relief, she continued to remain aloof and withdrawn, misery still dominating her relationships in general. One day after a discussion on sacramental confession, she went home and prayed for guidance. Reluctantly, she realized that this was something the Lord was telling her to do. But to one so timid it would be a terrific ordeal. At last she made the appointment and began to prepare herself by mentally going through her life, listing the things for which she wished to ask God's forgiveness. The list seemed to stretch longer and longer. Finally, the day came; and she knelt at the altar as she made her confession to God in the presence of our rector. He gave her some words of wise counsel and suggested the reading of Psalm 139 as her penance; then he pronounced God's absolution of her sins. She returned to the pew, read the Psalm and made her thanksgiving, feeling as if she had been spiritually purged.

Next day she felt like a different person; she had a new light-heartedness, an irresistible joy. To those prayer group friends who could not fail to notice new light in her eyes and joy that seemed to flood her whole being, she replied, "I feel as if I am really clean inside! It's as if I've had a bath, inside as well as outside." Jane's attitude toward her mother-in-law was changed and the older woman seemed to have no more power to disturb her. Problems in Jane's relationships began to be resolved until finally her husband was brought back into the home in which Christ had become the Head, where His Love flowed. This once timid and bitter young woman became a channel of God's love in her church choir. Later she received the baptism in the Holy Spirit and became a radiant, integrated person and a leader of the prayer group in which formerly she had once been too timid to say a word. Her power to witness, both spoken and unspoken, has been an important part of the spiritual rebirth in the parish. "Bless the Lord . . . who forgiveth all thine iniquities; who healeth all thy diseases; who redeemeth thy life from destruction; who crowneth thee with loving-kindness and tender mercies" (Psalm 103:2-4 A.V.).

If our Lord in His earthly ministry could heal a man of physical paralysis by pronouncing God's forgiveness of his sins, why cannot His Body the Church be used by God today to pronounce the forgiveness of sin and set free one who is spiritually and almost mentally paralyzed by fear or resentment and the guilt of these spiritual sins? We are told: "there is joy among the angels of God over one sinner who repents" (Luke 15:10). Is it not likely that the person repenting will experience some of this joy also? Dr. Carl Jung reports from case studies that Protestants appear to be more prone to mental illnesses than Roman Catholics, very possibly because often the former have not formed the habit of regular confession, cleansing of the soul of its accumulated burden of guilt. This is not to say that everyone must go to a priest, either Roman Catholic or Anglican, but it is being found by many psychiatrists today that guilt is the cause of a great part of the mental illness brought to their attention.

A non-Christian psychiatrist may try to explain away guilt to release the patient from his burden. On the contrary, a Christian psychiatrist wisely understands that only God can forgive sin and that repentance and confession are necessary to the deeper healing which can come when a burdened heart accepts personally God's forgiveness. A Christian psychiatrist may pray with his patient, or he may send him to his pastor or priest for confession so that the poison of guilt feelings will be cleansed. And through God's absolution (in whichever way it is pronounced) the patient receives the blessing of God's healing Peace. Very often physical healing follows this spiritual and mental healing so that the whole person is restored.

A young woman, a life-time member of the Episcopal Church, had never heard of sacramental confession. Ruth had been deeply hurt as a child by lack of love and it had made her a shy, rather suspicious person, one who because of her own memories of rejection had always found it difficult to give out love to others. Although she had seen what confession could do in the life of a friend (indeed she had been one of God's channels for the friend's healing of desperate, suicidal-tendency depression) Ruth had not applied the cure to herself. When finally she realized that it was the Holy Spirit convicting her (and not the members of our prayer group) she made an appointment with our rector. After having made her private confession to God in his presence, she returned home feeling quite weak from the deep cleansing of this experience. But in a few days she found that everything in her life was taking on different values. New strength and love so filled her that she vowed she would recommend this means of "spiritual housecleaning" to everyone. Her growth in God's grace was wonderful to behold as she became a more loving wife and mother. Eventually, she became the leader of a neighborhood prayer group and a person on whom our rector could depend for lay help in carrying out his pastoral work through the healing ministry in our church. She has been used by the Lord as a channel of healing to many, especially those in mental illness, and eventually to the one in her own family who for so long had painfully hurt her by a denial of love. Praise the Lord who alone can forgive sin and heal broken relationships!

The Bible clearly states: "If we claim to be sinless, we are self-deceived and strangers to the truth. If we confess our sins, he is just, and may be trusted to forgive our sins and cleanse us from every kind of wrong; but if we say we have committed no sin, we make him out to be a liar, and then his word has no place in us" (I John 1:8-10).

Holy Matrimony

In his Letter to the Ephesians, St. Paul describes the relationship in marriage as similar to that between Christ and His Body the Church, of which we are all living parts.

A young couple of different nationalities were joined together in Holy Matrimony but this was more than an ordinary marriage. Each of them had been seeking (even on distant shores) for the one to complete life. Each of them in the past had been hurt in such a way that an especially understanding mate was necessary. They were introduced by the Divine Providence of their loving Heavenly Father who suddenly answered their long-time prayers in a most complicated and unusual trans-Atlantic meeting—one only God could have arranged! In gratitude to Him, their engagement began, for in His Wisdom and Mercy He had spared them for each other and had drawn them together across thousands of miles. In deep joy they entered into the state of Holy Matrimony, aware that it is an estate ordained by God and symbolic of the "marriage" between Christ and His Church. Healing is God's gift to those who will receive it in gratitude; guidance comes to those who in humility are listening, those who are obedient, willing to be led. God's Will is for wholeness, and in this marriage they were made whole.

In a happy marriage the two persons involved find joy in *completing* each other—*not* competing with each other! The divine order in marriage is fulfilled when the wife is submissive to her husband as Christ is Head in him (I Cor. 11:3). It is very important that the husband and wife *pray together* for the Lordship of Jesus Christ in their home—not the lordship of either one of them or their children, as so often happens today. St. Paul's words are still valid: "Children, obey your parents in the Lord, for this is right . . . Fathers, do not provoke your children to anger, but bring them up in the discipline and instruction of the Lord" (Eph. 6:1,4, RSV). In Christian marriage, "a man shall leave his father and mother and be joined to his wife, and the two shall become one" (Eph. 5:31, RSV). Christ is to be the Head of the home—not the couple's parents; to honor one's parents does not mean "in-law domination"—which (no matter how well intentioned) often causes marital discord. St. Paul's advice is good today: "Let each one of you love his wife as himself, and let the wife see that she respects her husband" (Eph. 5:33, RSV).

HEALING THROUGH SACRAMENTS

My next step in healing was to realize that our Lord heals through the regular sacraments of His Church, not just at special services. A sacrament is "an outward and visible sign of an inward and spiritual grace." In my own personal experience I have found it necessary to seek the Source of all life at the altar as well as through medicine. Divine Healing is a *fact,* not just a theory.

The following experiences are related to illustrate God's Healing Power flowing through the two sacraments of the Church, Holy Communion and Holy Baptism. Space permits the recounting of only a few of many healings to which I can witness personally. It is hoped the reader will see that our Lord's visible ministry is continuous and available to those who will believe and call upon His Name today. The means vary but the Lord is the same: yesterday, today and forever. The Church is His healing Body and not a group of so-called "healers".

Healing Through Holy Baptism

An aged priest, retired because of failing health, was called upon because as yet no successor had come to be the rector of his former parish. A transient family had telephoned the church office, asking that he come to their caravan and give their dying baby the sacrament of Holy Baptism. They felt this was the last resort—all they could do for their precious little one. The priest answered the call in faith, even though it was a severe strain on his own health. And, because he could not return the next day, I was asked to visit the family.

The mother answered the doorbell and with a radiant face

exclaimed, "A miracle has happened!" There was the seven-month-old baby, sitting up in his high chair, a picture of health—waving his bottle in the air. Praise God from whom all blessings flow! Is it not a pity that so many Christians pay more attention to vaccinating their babies than to baptizing them?

A few months later the divorced mother of a nine-year-old girl called me in distress after doctors had held a week of tests in hospital and diagnosed the child's illness as rheumatic fever. The mother was forced to earn their living, so this news was doubly distressing. Although she had previously on occasions attended our prayer group and the child was enrolled in Sunday School, the climate of faith in this home was weak. The little girl had never been baptized. There was reason to believe that the child's illness could be related to her own sense of loss in not having a father's love and to the mother's bitter resentment against the father.

Our new young priest agreed to prepare the child for Holy Baptism, with the added intention of healing the lack of love in the relationships as well as physical healing. Two of us as members of the church volunteered to be godparents: a devout young man to fill the need for masculine concern, and I as leader of the prayer group. We were to represent the Love of the Body of Christ for this family on the fringe of the church. Thus, the child was made aware of the Love of her Heavenly Father; and the mother, of the Love of Christ and His Church in her time of loneliness and fear. The little girl co-operated well during convalescence, and she studied hard at home with the help of a visiting teacher to keep up with her class. A few months later, the doctors agreed that she had no symptoms of rheumatic fever. She was able to return to school and has since been confirmed in the Church. Praise be to the Living Christ who heals today!

Our Lord laid His hands on little children brought to Him. He even raised from the dead the daughter of Jairus. Many priests today have witnessed similar examples of the Living Christ's power to use the water of Holy Baptism for blessing and healing the unbaptized sick. One elderly priest after a long and consecrated ministry has even said that in every case where he baptized a supposedly dying child, it recovered.

God was thus glorified!

Healing Through Holy Communion

Gertrude was a married woman who had patiently borne the problems of a desperately unhappy marriage that apparently was at an end. Legally, the case for divorce was perfectly clear, and, humanly speaking, there seemed to be little point in going on with something injurious to the three young children because, owing to the husband's alcoholism and sadism, there was no safety in their home. Our rector had had many talks with her husband but to no apparent avail, and, although as a priest he could scarcely recommend divorce, he acknowledged that it seemed inevitable. As a member of our prayer group, Gertrude had prayed earnestly for several years and yet the relationship had become worse instead of better. It appeared to be God's permissive (though not intentional) Will for the marriage to be dissolved.

Because she felt that she could not sign the legal papers for divorce until she had some clear-cut guidance from God, Gertrude and I went together one morning to Holy Communion. Our rector also was making her decision a "special intention". At the altar, immediately after having received the bread and wine, this devout woman "felt" more than heard the words, "Believe that ye have received." It was not what she had consciously wanted to hear. She had really come in despair seeking confirmation of the decision to go ahead with the divorce proceedings. Instead, in obedience, she cancelled these plans. Her life gradually changed but not without many frustrating setbacks and very real hardships. There were times when her faith faltered and she would not have been able to go on except for the assurance of those unforgettable words and the sustaining love of the prayer fellowship. But because her love of the Lord was greater than her pride, and because her obedience to Him was greater than the desire for an easy way out, she continued to pray in faith, allowing Him to use her as a channel of His Love to the husband, forgiving till the seventh times seven. The healing of his alcoholism was the Lord's answer to her persistent prayers of faith.

Ten years later her husband again became abusive and his philandering made a divorce necessary, for he wilfully threw away the opportunity which God had given him. The delay in time had given the children a chance to grow older so that she could better support them. God had healed the husband of the desire for alcohol, but He did not take away his freedom of will. Because the husband misused this freedom of will, the "healing" proved to be a temporary remission. When the man again succumbed to adultery, the marriage had to be dissolved, but by God's grace the innocent parties were carried safely through the deep waters. Gertrude has since married a very fine man and her children now have the human father-love they so greatly need. One is reminded that Jesus said: "Sin no more, that nothing worse befall you" (John 5:14 RSV).

In His earthly ministry Jesus gave two parables illustrating the spiritual law of persistency in prayer. In both parables He was in effect saying that if human beings respond affirmatively to a persistent request, how much more will a just and loving Heavenly Father honor the continuing prayers of faith! In the case of the Canaanite woman who was begging for the healing of her daughter, Jesus seemed to withhold the healing until she had asked several times, probably because He was testing her humility and sincerity. This may be a reason for delayed answers to prayers; it may take time for the healing of her daughter, Jesus seemed to withhold the healing until she had asked several times, probably because He was testing her humility and sincerity. This may be a reason for delayed answers to prayers; it may take time for the healing Love of God to flow through human channels where it is difficult to forgive in sufficient force to affect a healing. Again it may be that man, who has been given freedom of will, can delay his response to the healing Love of Christ, even though the human channel is offering itself to God to be used redemptively. My friend's story related above illustrates suffering for the sin of the world—a true part of "bearing Christ's Cross".

Physical healing, too, is often experienced in Holy Communion. Once when weary from the ordeal of moving from a distant city I fell from a step-ladder and injured my back. Within a few hours I became very stiff, and all that day I was in agony. I prayed for the Lord's healing touch so that I could go on with the task of settling my family in our new home. The next morning I went to Holy Communion with physical healing as my "special intention". On returning to my pew I felt movement in my back as if an unseen Hand were adjusting the painful muscles and ligaments. I slipped to my knees in thanksgiving and in a few moments arose perfectly healed. A month or so later the Lord used me to start a prayer group in that church, in thanksgiving to share my faith with others who were seeking the experience of His healing power.

Our Lord said to the woman in the crowd who had only touched the hem of His robe, "My daughter, your faith has cured you" (Matthew 9:22). We must remember that faith is not just "faith in faith" or "faith in prayer" but rather "faith in the Person of Jesus Christ the Healer". He comes to those who believe in His Real Presence today—under the forms of the bread and wine in the Holy Eucharist (Thanksgiving). As the minister says the words "Preserve thy *body and soul"*, we can trustingly put ourselves in God's Hands and pray for His Highest Gift—the Gift of His Indwelling Spirit. Then we can leave the altar expectantly, thankfully, trusting the details to Him.

Healing of bereavement has also often been found at Holy Communion. Deborah, an unmarried older woman, had depended greatly on her mother who was a member of a school of Christianity that did not express its faith through the sacraments. When her mother died she was completely bereft and physically crippled. Friends brought her for the laying-on of hands and prayer group each Wednesday morning. Their love was a channel for the Lord so she continued to come each week, drawn as by a magnet to the altar. But her sense of loss and heartbreaking loneliness for her mother were not mitigated by other human love, no matter how much it was appreciated. Deborah was baptized and confirmed and her physical healing continued. One morning, while receiving the sacrament, her mother's love became unexpectedly real to her in a wonderful and indescribable way. It was as if God had allowed Deborah this priceless moment to reassure her that her beloved mother was truly "alive in Christ". In the Communion of Saints, at Christ's own altar, they were reunited in His Spirit and the daughter *knew* that His healing Love would link them together until some day she would rejoin her mother in the Larger Life. This profound and unforgettable experience of the mercy of the Lord healed her sense of bereavement. Although she continued to miss her mother's physical presence, Deborah had been through her own personal "death and resurrection". She was eager to glorify God as a new person in Christ Jesus.

While attending confirmation classes she met a fine young couple who "adopted" her as if she were their own mother; and so the Lord fulfilled her need for a family, giving her a heart-warming personal relationship, as well as the very real sense of being part of the "Family in Christ", the Church. On Easter Day she walked unaided to the altar. She wore a corsage given by the young man—a duplicate of his gift to his wife. And when the couple went on holiday that summer, Deborah was privileged to go with them. She became a serenely radiant person, a channel of Christ's healing power to others.

We are reminded that our Lord (when told that His mother and brothers were waiting to speak to Him) replied, pointing to the disciples, "Here are my mother and my brothers. Whoever does the will of my heavenly Father is my brother, my sister, my mother" (Matthew 12:50). St. Paul wrote in his first Letter to the Corinthians: "For Christ is like a single body with its many limbs and organs, which, many as they are, together make up one body. For indeed we were all brought into one body by baptism, in the one Spirit, whether we are Jews or Greeks, whether slaves or free men, and that one Holy Spirit was poured out for all of us to drink. A body is not one single organ, but many . . . Now you are Christ's body, and each of you a limb or organ of it" (12:12-14, 27).

AVENUES TO HEALING

The sick have a part to play in their healing along with the physician. As we saw in the last chapter, it is necessary to cleanse our hearts of the sins of fear, resentment, pride, self-pity and the like. There are many avenues of prayer that can make us more open to receive the wholeness that God wills for us. In some cases we need the help of others, especially when we are so bound by the past that we cannot deliver ourselves from its crippling effect on our lives. But all of these higher roads lead to deeper commitment to our Lord.

Job faced the problem of suffering, and his friends offered their advice. The real message of the story is this: when catastrophes or illnesses come into our lives we are not to wallow in self-pity nor become morbid in self-accusation or that of others, but rather to fix our eyes on God and ask Him to teach us how to grow in spiritual discipline and in awareness of Himself.

We need to adopt an attitude of surrender to Jesus who can bring good out of evil through His Power, Wisdom and Love revealed in the Cross. When we trust in Him as our Risen Savior and surrender to Him as "Resident Boss" of our lives, His healing touch can change our hearts and the situations around us. Conversion can happen in a moment but sanctification (bringing forth the fruit of the Spirit) is a lifetime's work.

Conversion

In the beginning of his book, Dr. Loring T. Swaim writes that it is essential to know and understand the teaching of Jesus: "His spiritual laws are as inexorable as physical laws." He then summarizes these teachings as "the law of love", "the law of apology", "the law of change", "the law of fault-finding" and "the law of forgiveness".[1]

Eleven years before I read this dedicated doctor's book, its lessons were learned in "the school of hard knocks". I was extremely active in Christian work, assisting my rector in the phenomenally rapid growth of his new mission Church, doing parish visiting, setting up the women's work and the Sunday School as well as much of the secretarial work. I was doing all the right things but too often with the wrong attitudes. Tension was building up within me, partly because of my own perfectionism and the never-ending pressure of the work. My attitude was critical and self-righteous toward those who were not shouldering the load with me. Smouldering within me was a deep resentment toward one who had rejected me many years before.

I had vowed then that I would never again let anyone hurt me. Often I had thought I was winning the victory over my feelings but a fresh reminder always brought out another wave of resentment. Other hostile feelings seemed to spread out from this long-standing grudge; like weeds in a garden, it flourished underground only to crop up in new places.

While under the pressure of winding up my church work and making advance preparations for our move to Japan, I developed severe headaches and vertigo. The doctor diagnosed it as infection of the middle ear, gave me three kinds of pills, and told me it would probably take six months for me to be well enough to make the trip. Alas, I had less than three months before my sailing date! Either I made that port-call or our plans to move to Japan would be cancelled.

With a real sense of urgency I felt God's guidance to go to a CFO retreat. Arriving late, I was just in time for the afternoon prayer group at the end of which the leader, a laywoman, laid hands on me for healing. As I rose from the chair, it seemed as if my ears were opened up in a wonderful way. My headache vanished immediately. I had been healed within two hours of my arrival—physically, that is!

Although I was ready to go home—or so I thought—it seemed that the Lord was keeping me there. A fine young Methodist minister talked to me about Jesus, and somehow I knew that I wanted the closeness he had found. To my then narrow-minded attitude it was unthinkable that there were only four Episcopalians at this spiritual retreat. Most were Methodists, Presbyterians, Baptists.

The last afternoon a prison evangelist came to speak to us of her work and we asked her to tell us how she talked to those who had been converted under her ministry. I must have *really* heard the Gospel for the first time, for afterwards I ran to the prayer chapel alone and knelt before its little altar. In my heart I "saw" Jesus dying on the Cross for me. I was convicted of my sins of hatred which our Lord condemned as murder in the spirit. I saw through my spiritual eyes that I had nailed Him to the Cross—I, who had been a pillar of my church, had crucified Him with my resentments, my self-pity, my fears, pride, self-righteousness and critical spirit! My tears seemed never to end as my heart literally cried out in repentance for the spiritual sins that had been nails in His Cross. Then, as suddenly, a great Peace filled my heart. I did not need to see a vision; I *knew* that Jesus was Lord of my heart and mind and soul and body. At last I was free to be the person He had created me to be.

When finally I left the chapel, a wave of Joy and Love overwhelmed me. I felt that I was a "new person in Christ Jesus". Other people evidently could see the change too, and they rejoiced with me that I had found Jesus as my personal Savior from the bondage of the sins of the spirit. I could now love all those whom I could not love previously.

Life took on a new dimension. Two weeks after my return home, our daughter said, "Mama, you are so much nicer to live with." Although the headaches returned temporarily whenever I broke the spiritual laws, I had only to repent quickly with a silent "arrow prayer" of: "Lord, forgive me. I've done it again. Help me to overcome this fear (or resentment or pride)." I had only to press against my right temple as I prayed silently: "Lord, heal me and help me to do better." The headache would be instantly lifted. It was as if the Lord had given me a "built-in alarm clock" to remind me when I was spiritually off the track!

The Kingdom Way is narrow and straight but our Lord in His Mercy is ever-ready to forgive and help His erring children to find it once more. Gradually it became easier to "walk in the Spirit" of Love as the old self-centered thought habits gave way to the new Jesus-centered attitude toward life. A wonderful Savior is Jesus our Lord!

In *Beyond Commitment,* my friend the Rev. Ben C. Johnson writes: "As He fills our minds with love, even to love the unlovely, we are finding release from the crippling power of resentment. And in reality we are finding that we no longer are the center of the universe—He is! From self to Christ, and what a relief to have the burden of control off our hands."[2]

Surrender

We try to surrender our problems to God. Why do we so often fail? Because our real need is to surrender *ourselves,* not just our problems. If our surrender is such that we can truthfully say, "Living or dying makes no difference", then our problems will cease to be problems, for to such a great extent they are within us. It is not really vital whether the day is rainy or sunny, but the way we accept this is important. We are not necessarily joyous when life runs smoothly, nor are we necessarily sad when life's problems are great. To the extent that we are surrendered to God we can have His Joy regardless of the conditions within which we find ourselves.

One of the highest principles of prayer (and one of the hardest to practice) is that of surrender, and yet it is the main road to inner peace: for in *His* Will is *our* Peace! A few years ago on my return journey to England I was able to spend only one day in a city where I had many Christian friends who had arranged for me to lead a "Day Apart with God". There was also a church speaking engagement that evening and a steady stream of counselling appointments with people with desperate problems. On arrival I learned that there was absolutely no time to visit two friends, each of whom was critically ill but in distant hospitals. One had a serious heart condition and the other had had a radical cancer operation of which her doctor had said, "We can only hope for the best." My heart was very much with them both, and I found it extremely difficult to pray the prayer of surrender, yet I knew that it was the only way I could really help them. After a period of contemplative meditation on the Love of God, I felt that at last I could mean it when I prayed, "Living or dying makes no difference, Lord. I release them to You, knowing that You will do whatever is *best* in these situations. Thank you, Lord, that I can give them both to You."

The tremendous sense of Peace that followed this time of prayer was one I had known when praying for our son's healing of a malignancy some years before. After that, it was easy to hold these two friends up to God in short prayers throughout the day as one would put a potted plant in a sunny window to catch the life-giving warmth of the rays. It seemed right just to "think and thank" God that they belonged to Him, so there was nothing to fear. It was easy to include the nurses and doctors, the families and friends in the circle of His Love which by prayer was being placed around these two Christians whose greatest desire was to glorify Jesus. Several months later, letters confirmed that both of them were healed and grateful to be returned to useful lives—far beyond their doctors' expectations! Many, many other prayers had also been offered for them, each one a channel for our Lord's healing power to flow into their beings. What a blessing it is to be allowed by God to co-operate in His healing work! He has given us freedom of will but we must freely surrender that will—of our own volition, give it back—to Him.

Thanksgiving

Thanksgiving is another essential avenue of prayer. Even when God closes one door we can thank Him that He will open another and better one! St. Paul admonished the Philippians to give thanks in *everything* as they made their requests to God. About the time our first child was born I developed very severe hay fever. Exhaustive tests proved that my paroxysms of sneezing were a result of allergy to several foods, house dust, molds and especially ragweed. I had to take a series of immunizations each summer before the ragweed season began. Even so, my distress was sufficiently great that I almost wished I could die from it! Sleepless nights and prolonged spasms of sneezing left me not only red-eyed but also exhausted by day. There is no medical cure for hay fever.

Ten years later I was guided to go to a CFO retreat, instead of taking the usual anti-histamines or injections. I felt assurance that God would heal me in that faith-charged atmosphere where His Love created a spiritual climate for healing. After waiting five days, nothing had happened; and in my "quiet time" early that morning I asked the Lord to show me why. To my amazement His reply flashed through my mind, "You have not *thanked* Me." My own ingratitude and lack of expectancy were evidently the blocks to fulfilment of His Will. I asked Him to forgive me and began to praise Him in advance of my healing. Throughout the morning while participating in the day's activities, an undercurrent of thanksgiving filled my heart. At noon I suddenly realized that I had not sneezed for several hours! The day wore on and night came and still there were no wearying symptoms. After a good night's sleep, I awakened refreshed, praising my Savior and Healer.

Several years ago at the very hour my rector and I arrived at a healing retreat in a distant city, a member of our Prayer Group telephoned to ask for immediate prayers as her young daughter, Joan, had encephalitis. We claimed the healing Love of Christ surrounding the family and visualized Him touching the little girl with His healing Power. A very real wave of thanksgiving swept away all doubt and fear from our hearts and we continued to praise the Lord each time we thought of Joan, as we eagerly awaited a telephone call to confirm the healing already accepted in our spirits. The next day the mother's voice exclaimed over the telephone, "It's a miracle! Joan is perfectly well! I've had the strangest feeling—as if I were packed in cotton wool. I just couldn't worry about her. In fact, I even went out on the balcony yesterday to sit down to worry because I couldn't worry!" This was a double miracle, for the mother had always been given to excessive worrying about her children. Now she makes a sign of the Cross on their foreheads as she prays a morning prayer with them before they go off to school. And she leaves them in God's hands.

Consecrating the Imagination

One of God's natural gifts to man is the imagination.

Unfortunately, we more often *mis*-use it! A consecrated imagination is one trained to see life as God wants it to be—with eyes of faith. When disease strikes, most people allow their imaginations to run wild in a negative way instead of holding the situation up to God in a positive way.

Years ago during an epidemic the grandson of a very well-known spiritual leader was stricken with polio and spinal meningitis. Believing that doubt-filled prayers are useless and that fearful thoughts are destructive, she called fifty of her prayer group friends, only those on whom she could rely for prayers of *real faith* in medically incurable situations. We were asked to tell no one else about this illness and to pray as often as possible throughout the day: "Thank you, Lord, that You are healing Harry in the way You know is best." Once each hour we were to visualize the little seven-year-old boy playing ball as he loved to do.

We had the faith to hold Harry in this spiritual climate; to let God use our imaginations constructively, as a shield of faith to protect him from the usual thoughts of fear and pity surrounding him in hospital. Within twenty-four hours Harry was out of isolation. It was easy to continue our prayers with great thanksgiving. Two days later the doctor told the parents in the presence of their rector that the child showed definite post-polio and spinal meningitis symptoms, adding that he must have been healed by a Higher Power. Within a week, Harry was home from the hospital, and soon afterward he was playing ball, just as we had visualized him. Praise the Lord!

Because of this experience I was guided to pray similarly when our thirteen-year-old son had a malignant tumor on the thyroid gland. Although I had complete faith that God would heal him, twenty-six doctors on the Tumor Board insisted on the operation. My husband and I agreed to it because their many tests and X-rays indicated the need for immediate removal of the malignant tumor. We had asked our rector to have a private healing service following Holy Communion on the Sunday before the operation. Owing to the extent and nature of this growth, the surgeons found it necessary to remove three quarters of the thyroid gland as well as the egg-sized tumor. Ordinarily I would have been fearful at this more serious extent of the operation except for the assurance that the Lord had truly touched Richard through our faith at the altar. When four different pathologists sent back the verdict "Negative", the doctors on the Tumor Board of this large Naval Hospital felt there must be some mistake. They had been certain enough of their diagnosis to remove not only the malignant tumor but also three quarters of the thyroid gland! As one half is necessary for normal body functioning, they warned us that thyroid supplements would be needed to make up this deficiency. Further biopsies were made and sent away—only to be returned with the same (amazing to them) diagnosis.

The doctors insisted that the cells had been malignant; and that for some freak reason (possibly because of his youth) this did not show up on these tests but would reappear later. So monthly check-ups were required. Their negative comments were depressing, and my faith seemed to be particularly necessary to insulate Richard from the fears projected on him because they expected their original diagnosis to be reconfirmed. Often as I looked at his sailing boat perched on its trailer outside the kitchen window, my heart was inclined to waver and wonder if he would sail it again. At such times I found it helpful to visualize Richard sailing his beloved boat. To this mental picture, I added one of him as an acolyte serving at the altar of our church.

Months passed. Richard began to grow taller and stronger. We continued to thank God for His healing power as our son was by then leading a very active life, playing football and tennis. There was no sign of recurrence of the malignancy and none of the "sluggishness" that the doctors had predicted because of thyroid deficiency. He was taking no thyroid supplement. That summer Richard joined the sailing classes at the Yacht Club. After a newspaper reporter took pictures of their various activities for young people, our paper printed a picture of him sailing his boat, just as I had been imagining it for the past three months! A few years later he became the senior acolyte in our Church. And in his last year of school he won a scholarship for the university of his choice. Physically, spiritually and mentally he was anything but "sluggish", yet he had been given no thyroid supplement!

Four years after the operation, during a check-up the doctors noted a difference in the area of his thyroid gland. They made a geiger counter test after first having given him the "atomic cocktail". To their amazement and our joy, the test revealed that the remaining one quarter segment of his thyroid gland had developed perfectly into a half, and that is all a person really needs. Thanks be to God who changed the nature of the cells and even restored the deficiency caused by the operation! Twelve years later Richard is working toward his Ph.D. degree in Physiological Psychology specializing in brain research. He has done all of his post-graduate work under fellowships or research assistantships and is far from being "sluggish"!

Contemplative Meditation

During my last year in London, I was privileged to experience this form of healing meditation in an elderly minister's class. He radiated so much of the Love and Peace of Jesus that I was eager to study his approach to healing. In our world of anxiety and fear we need to set aside time for contemplative meditation, to let God's Truth sink deep within our subconscious minds to dissolve tensions.

A motivational researcher analyzed religious belief thus: "If your faith is grounded in the subconscious mind, it will sustain you through any crisis. If it is no deeper than your conscious mind, it will desert you the moment you are off guard or under pressure. I believe that this explains a great deal of the moral illness with which our society is afflicted ... The moment that the subconscious mind does accept a belief, it begins organizing all its powers toward putting it into effect, and its God-given power is amazing. Jesus Christ knew all about the subconscious mind and the part it played in our lives." In Psalm 64:6b we read: "For the inward mind and heart of a man are deep!"

This is why it is so important for us not to dwell on thoughts of pain or weakness, for by doing so we help to create those unhappy conditions in our bodies. For me, one of the most helpful meditations is "Be still and *know* that I am God and *take hold of My Peace* within you." Try slowly and quietly saying these words, holding the thought silently until it begins to fade from the mind. Then repeat the words until the thought has been held for five or more minutes. As a daily practice, this is one way to dissolve tension so that the fruit of the Spirit can grow more real in our experience. One can substitute the words "Joy" or "Love" or "Patience". And in times of weakness I have found it helpful to use the word "Power" instead of "Peace". To begin and end the day thus is a healing therapy.

Some of us have found that in our time of deep meditation on God's Peace, we can lift a sick person through very real intercession, as our faith becomes the channel for God's Grace to flow into the one in need. We can *believe for them* until they find faith of their own to believe in Jesus' Resurrection Power. During a friend's illness at about nine o'clock one evening, I could literally feel tension coming from her like a wave of darkness. As it was too late to go to see her, I lifted her name into the Peace that followed a few minutes of meditation. After holding it for twenty minutes I then felt released. The next day she told me that she had suffered a severe nervous spell, but at about nine-twenty it lifted and she had soon fallen asleep.

Prayer is a way by which the Healing Christ enters and transforms our lives and, through us, the lives of others. God's power is unlimited, but we often limit it in our consciousness, in our narrowed horizons, when His mercy is as great as the ocean!

We can find wholeness only by inward reconciliation with God, not just on the conscious, intellectual level but also on the subconscious level. As we appropriate His forgiveness we bring to bear on our specific needs Christ's Peace and redeeming Love. The Bishop of Lincoln in dedicating a home of healing in England said, "Forgiveness is the gift of the life of Christ for healing and wholeness at the point in our life where we know of our need." At the close of the service he left with us this prayer: "Lord, forgive what we have been, sanctify what we are, order what we shall be. What we know not, teach us. What we have not, give us. What we are not, make us, for Christ's sake, Amen."

X

BARRIERS TO HEALING

There are no favorites in God's Providence, but there are often conditions which need to be met because Divine Healing is not magic. My quest to know more of the avenues of healing led me to analyze those in which I had been involved. As I searched my own heart and the experiences of others, it became very clear that in many avoidable ways a sick person can hinder the healing God is working in him.

This is not to say that God never heals unless the conditions are perfect. No one can limit the work of the Holy Spirit, and healings have occurred in some of the most unlikely cases. But it is to say that we have no right as Christians to ask God to break His spiritual laws because, for example, we do not want to give up a cherished resentment or grudge, our self-pity or pride. Intercession is not for the purpose of changing God—converting Him to our will—but rather for the changing of conditions within and around the patient to make them conform to God's Will. Too often we pray for God to heal an ulcer, but He says, "Let Me heal your relationships first." Sometimes we walk away.

Sometimes there are barriers—spiritual conditions that block healing in the patient, but there may well be similar hindrances in ourselves, although we, through prayer, are presumed to be the channels of Christ's healing Power. At other times there are obvious "spiritual short-circuits" in the families of patients. Sometimes a patient is suffocated spiritually by the negative attitudes of doctors and nurses who, lacking faith, see only the medical prognosis. They do not believe that "What is impossible for men is possible for God" (Luke 18:27). Most deplorable is the situation when the minister and congregation (who are supposed to be the

Body of Christ) are so lacking in faith that they actually project their negative fears and doubts onto the sick person. A man who had been healed by God of ulcers wondered why he felt worse when he went to the meeting of the Men's Club of his Church, whereas when he went to a prayer group he felt well. Thoughts such as "I wonder how much longer the old boy is going to last" were evidently making an impact upon his sensitive spirit, discouraging him in a way that is quite understandable to those who have been victims of this particular brand of "pity". Fortunately, in the prayer group there was an attitude of expectancy, of thanksgiving for improvement already noted. This was making a channel to complete healing of the man's mind and spirit as well as of his body. The sick one recovers more quickly when home, hospital and Church provide a spiritual climate of faith.

It is not difficult to see why God's healing Love had no effective channel into the life of a woman dying of leukemia, while her husband and mother were constantly bickering over her, even disputing the final future resting place of her body! In a similar instance, a well-known channel of God's healing power refused to pray and lay hands on a little child for healing of leukemia until the parents reconciled their bitter resentments toward each other, asking God's forgiveness for depriving *His* child of the much-needed "climate" of a loving home. God lends children to parents to be nurtured, not to be victims of their parents' tug-of-war. It was a mockery to ask God for healing when the child's "loved ones" were unwilling even to try to meet His conditions of Love. As a result of this insistence, the parents were reconciled. Intercessors must all be reminded that it is useless to expect God to break His spiritual laws.

Sometimes the channel of prayer is well-intentioned and loving but too weak and intermittent in faith. It may be rather like trying to pull a heavy cart with a thin strand of string, when a person "of little faith" takes on an advanced stage of cancer as an initial prayer project. This could lead to spiritual pride. Our Lord carefully trained His disciples before He sent them out to preach the Kingdom of God and heal the sick. They lived with Him and learned from Him by being in His Presence. This gives us the clues that effective prayer is not "natural" or easy for human beings, and that "practicing the Presence of God" is a very necessary part of praying for the sick. One does not just read a book and become an expert. Prayer is an art of which the Spirit is our Teacher; we often learn the hard way from our mistakes and failures. Sometimes we need to pray to know if we are lagging behind or going ahead of His time-table in speaking to others about prayer. Strangely enough, intelligent men and women, who would not think of playing a piano or practicing a profession without years of intensive study, seem to think that they are born knowing all there is to know about prayer, or that they have learned it in Sunday School, or that they have absorbed it by association with others.

The sick person in his weakness often has to depend on the faith of his friends or family or church to support him with their prayers. One could compare these prayers to the tube through which the patient is fed intravenously—a spiritual feeding. If the faith is faltering, the patient is deprived of a steady flow of God's healing Love. It is, of course, our Lord who heals. He uses the prayers of others than the sick today, just as He did in the case of the Roman centurion who interceded for his servant or the Syrophoenician woman who begged help for her child. We need to pray that the Holy Spirit will reveal any spiritual hindrances existing in ourselves and in those for whom we pray. Then these "interferences" can be offered up to our Lord for forgiveness and removal, to accelerate His healing work.

Resentments

It is useless to go to a doctor to heal our ulcers, if we are not willing to give up our worries or resentments. A Christian doctor once told of admonishing a patient: "You must cut out your resentments, or I will have to cut out a part of your intestinal tract." Stunned, the man replied that he had come to the office to be made well—not for a sermon! The doctor sent him home to think it over and told him to come back in two weeks. The patient thought a great deal about this advice. Finally, he decided to go to see a former business partner against whom he had been holding a very bitter grudge. To his relief, the partner admitted the wrong, promised redress, and their friendship was restored. When the patient returned for further examination the physician found the condition healed. If this man had not given up the resentment, which was the "spiritually unresolved shock", the operation might have been successful, it is true. But the chances of recurrence would have been great. Instead of just getting well, this man was made whole.

When the source of poison is removed, as in this case of forgiving reconciliation, with God's Grace the mind and spirit can co-operate in physical healing. The "acid" of deep-seated grudges no longer affects the organs of the body. We human beings "poison" ourselves with our unhealthy emotions which release glandular fluids, for example, adrenalin in time of great fear. Over a period of time this can cause functional illness which, given long enough, can become organic. Many physicians on both sides of the Atlantic have assured me that the human body is affected by disturbed thoughts and negative emotions, such as anger, jealousy, self-pity, guilt and deep-seated fears. In turn, the symptoms so caused in the body tend to reinforce these aggravated attitudes of the mind and soul—a "vicious circle". Although originally the following illnesses were considered to have only physical, "organic" causes, in recent years many doctors have noted the importance of treating the patient's mind and emotions—not just the body. Many notable cures have been medically documented of such diseases as: asthma, hay-fever and other allergies; hypertension, digestive ulcers and ulcerative colitis; certain forms of heart disease and cancer; bursitis, tendonitis and rheumatoid arthritis.

Often a doctor says to an ulcer patient, "Don't worry over everything." He is asking the patient to stop a habit that probably is life-long and beyond his ability to control. But God in His Love can transform fear, anxiety, resentment, jealousy, pride, guilt and the other illness-causing emotions into healthy ones of trust, peace, love, humility and forgiveness. God alone can revolutionize the human heart by changing its motives. He can and does make men whole today. As our self-will yields to God's Will, He gives us the Power to be changed.

In *Love or Perish,* the late Dr. Smiley Blanton wrote on

the basis of observation made during more than forty years of practice as a psychiatrist. Urging on mankind the way of love, he pointed out the destructive power of hate and the health-creating force of love within those who had formerly been victims of their emotions.

Fear

Pastor Robert Forget in *The Way to Divine Healing* has drawn up a "Table of Correspondences" based on many hundreds of cases he has observed in his ministry in France. He writes, for example, "The liver is attacked by fear, pre-occupation. The heart is attacked by fear, emotional shocks. The skin is attacked by anxiety, worry. The gallbladder is attacked by bitterness, jealousy. The nerves are attacked by emotional shocks. Eczema may be caused by suppression, inhibited desires. Rheumatism may be caused by bitterness, grudges."[1] One is reminded of common expressions that relate emotions to illness, such as, "She makes me sick at my stomach" or "He gives me a headache".

A very attractive woman went to her doctor for a routine check-up and was terrified when he discovered a tumor. Although he assured Lucy that it was benign and there was no cause to fear, she paid no attention to his words. Fear of cancer possessed her. She was sure that she was not being told the truth. The doctor felt that her preoccupation with cancer influenced the development of malignant cells. Finally, her husband (who had very great faith) persuaded her, rather against her own inclination, to allow our prayer group to visit and pray with her. After each visit her intake of drugs markedly decreased for at least twenty-four hours, but it seemed as if Lucy's fearful obsession was a barrier and ultimately cancelled the effectiveness of prayers. She was unable to make a real response of faith, although finally, she joined the Church, mostly to please her family. As she grew daily weaker and in great pain, her husband held fast in faith and love, but nothing seemed to remove Lucy's deep-seated fear. One morning when her condition was very poor, a remarkable burst of joy suddenly took possession of her as her face became radiant with a new Light. Her devoted husband thought that she was going to be physically healed at last. After a beautiful, comforting half-hour together, she quietly drew a deep breath as her earthly life ended. Although Lucy had never been able to accept with faith God's healing Love, He had touched her with His Joy and Peace which enabled her husband to have these brief happy memories. He had the assurance that although she had not recovered physically, Lucy was at last spiritually healed. Having already entered into the Joy of the Lord as she stood on the threshold of the Larger Life, her spirit departed to the Paradise our Lord has promised for those who believe in Him.

Although we pray for wholeness and life because they are God's gifts entrusted to us, nevertheless we must at all times remember that to a Christian, death is the doorway into the Larger Life, for which this life is only a place of preparation. For the Christian who has been prayed for and has at last received peace in this world, it is the final healing. We do not think of crutches and cancer existing in Paradise, but rather of Peace and Joy! *We* may prefer a different result. But if our attitude towards death is really Christian, we know that Christ promised that "There are many dwelling-places in my Father's house; if it were not so, I should have told you; for I am going there on purpose to prepare a place for you. And if I go and prepare a place for you, I shall come again and receive you to myself, so that where I am, you may be also" (John 14:2,3). If we truly love Christ, we can feel joy at being received by Him in the place He has prepared for us. If we are really unselfish, we will be glad for our loved ones to receive the Christian's reward of joy, although we ourselves may miss their human presence. In short, as Christians we are to "fight the good fight" of life with all our might because God has given us a purpose here, remembering at the same time that Christ is our prize. He was not defeated when He was put to death on a Cross; He turned death into eternal life! This applies to all who put their trust in Him, thus receiving this most precious gift of eternal life, now and forever.

In his newspaper column, Dr. Billy Graham has urged that those who are afraid of death should read I Corinthians 15. He points out that death has lost its sting for the Christian who, having confessed his sins and received Christ's forgiveness, trusts in Him into whose Presence he has been prepared to go. Psalm 23 committed to memory helps to fill the subconscious mind with faith, replacing fear. "Even though I walk through the valley of the shadow of death, I fear no evil; for thou art with me; thy rod and thy staff, they comfort me" (RSV). To hold this thought in one's mind helps to dissolve fear of death.

None of us can give easy answers to all questions concerning our Lord's healing Power, either today or in His earthly ministry. God still works in mysterious ways and His ways are not always our choices. Although we do not understand all His purposes, we go on believing and acting upon our faith, and, as we obey, it seems that we become clearer in our understanding. We *obey* because we are *committed to Him*, not because we understand!

Jealousy

An equally crippling emotion is jealousy. It seems to hurt the victim far more than the one who is possessed by jealousy. A young man who all his life had suffered because of his father's jealousy wrote to his mother on his twenty-first birthday following a wonderfully transforming experience of God's love:

"I can only send you thanks and love and further words of gratefulness for holding your marriage together until both Dad and I matured enough to love one another and thus break the spell of jealousy, fear, resentment and hatred. They had bound me for so long, held me so tightly, that I could not really love. And the love I gave even then was so terribly incomplete. As I could love only so slightly, I could not realize I had a soul, for the realization of one's soul comes with the realization of love. Childhood did not give me this knowledge of love, but rather the knowledge of hate, resentment, fear and bitterness. This, however, was through no fault of yours—do not blame yourself for it—for your love was all that kept me going at times. With the spell broken and myself free emotionally, I turn now to take care of my soul. I only hope you will *know* how much my love is with you, and my eternal gratefulness!"

Only the Grace of God had sustained this distressed

mother through the bitter feud between father and son. Like a sword at her heart for many years, it had been dividing their home as enmity poisoned all their relationships. Only God's Divine Love could have dissolved those crippling emotions which had bound two people she loved. Persistent prayers of faith were at last answered in the healing of the relationship between her husband and son. Although the clock could not be turned back to compensate for all the wasted years, this father and son could let the forgiveness of Christ heal the past as they began at last a new and more understanding relationship in His Love.

Possessive Love

Possessive love can be lust for power in disguise! It is a cruel parody of the real thing. It is love of self at the expense of the victim who is supposed to be the object of this perverted love. Dr. Smiley Blanton has pointed out that sometimes the person who has been dominated by a possessive mother becomes afraid of all entangling relationships. For some persons, "Smother love" is not a joke but a distressing reality. Once I felt led to pray for a mother of three children to be set free through the healing of the old scars from bondage to childhood fears of her intolerably oppressive mother. During the prayers she wept copiously and finally said, "I feel as if I'm growing up." The chains of the past were severed so that she would not project the same oppressive love on to her own children. By the grace of God the young woman was given wisdom to get a true perspective of herself before she damaged irreparably her relationships with her own children. She was able to forgive her mother and recognize her mother's insecurity as a result of her childhood domination.

When our daughter was growing up, I was frustrated because she would not conform to the way of life I had unconsciously chosen for her. In her middle teens she became more self-assertive and aggressive. A formerly happy relationship was about to founder on the reefs of conflicting interests and wills. Fortunately, God convicted me that, as a Christian, I needed to see my own sin in this unhappy situation, not just our daughter's rebellion. I was shown during self-examination (before making a sacramental confession) that I had been trying to force her to follow in my own footsteps—to go to the same college, to fit the same spiritual and intellectual mold, to conform to my ideas—instead of allowing her to mature according to her own capacities. She needed to exercise her God-given freedom of will to make these choices as *He* guided her. One day I went to Church, made my confession and accepted some wise advice from my rector. He gave me as my Penance the reading of Psalm 51, and I knelt in the pew beseeching the Lord to "renew a right spirit within" my heart. On returning home, great Peace filled my whole being. Half-an-hour later, Maryanna came in from school and greeted me as warmly as in former days, and from that moment onward, there seemed to be a new harmony in our relationship. She became remarkably thoughtful and appreciative as I explained to her my change of attitude and urged her to use her new freedom wisely with God's guidance. We are today exceptionally close, even though she is married and living permanently far away from us. She recently commented while introducing me to one of her contemporaries: "I love her as my mother—but even more I like her as a friend!" Distance does not separate us from those we love when we can surrender them to Christ.

Pride

While returning from a prayer group where as leader I had stressed the danger of holding injured pride and resentments, Elsie remarked airily, "Oh, I don't have any!" Next morning the Holy Spirit revealed to her that beneath the show of love toward her daughter-in-law were injured pride, self-righteousness and a deeply buried resentment because of the younger woman's excessive drinking. Elsie prayed earnestly about this. She asked the Lord to forgive her for spiritual pride, for judging her daughter-in-law and for being a hypocrite in pretending to love the young woman. Then she thanked Jesus for giving her honesty with herself and *His* Love. Humbly she prayed that a way might be revealed to show forth His Power to help her son's wife overcome this weakness. One night a few weeks later, God opened up the way for Elsie to go to the daughter-in-law's rescue, to stand with her in love when no one else would accept her because she had "disgraced" them. The next morning the two women had a heart-searching talk which could have taken place only because the daughter-in-law now knew for a fact the sincerity and humility of Elsie's love for her. They prayed together that Jesus would take control of the previously uncontrolled craving for strong drink and make His transforming Presence very real in the young woman's heart and home. For a Christian to show the Love of Jesus is not to condone the sin; we may hate the sin, but not the sinner! Our Lord Himself warned us against judging.

It has been my privilege to know the Rev. Ben C. Johnson and to be invited as a "High Church Methodist" to work in the Methodist Church with their Renewal through Lay Witnessing Missions. He writes in his challenging book, *Beyond Commitment:* "To love the unlovely is not human nature, but it is Christlikeness. Granted, this expression of love does not come from our willing, our striving, or our self-condemnation when we fail. This love is the outflow of a life that has found its center in the love of God; it is the expression of a life that has been claimed by the Lord Jesus Christ. When we once have looked at ourselves as we really are, our hard egoism is shattered by his amazing love to us. Then when we realize that God loves every other man just as he loves us, our judgment is softened, our barriers fall down, and we begin to love as he loves."[2] This is a great need in the lives about us today; to hear "God loves you, and I love you" is life-changing!

Self-Pity, Ingratitude and Gluttony

In my prayer counselling work I have seen many people who are struggling with the sin of gluttony. They over-eat compulsively, not so much from greed as from their own self-pity, rejection and insecurity. Then they berate themselves for gaining weight, and the problem usually becomes aggravated. When steeped in self-pity and insecurity, one feeds on the injury—and usually finds solace in food to compensate. The antidote for self-pity is thanksgiving. It is really not what happens to us but rather how we take it that makes the difference. The *way we accept* the stings of life affects our personalities. Self-pity expects the worst in a situation. Ingratitude is the twin of self-pity—for both fail to look for God's blessings. No situation is beyond the merciful Love of God, so ingratitude is a sin against the Holy Spirit.

Life had taken a sudden and very exhausting turn for Alice. Unexpected pressures seemed to crush her physically at a time of middle age when she needed to relax more. Prolonged and severe emotional complications added to the strain of moving her family to a new city. She felt depleted and overtaxed mentally, emotionally and physically. Self-pity had entered the door of her heart, and although conscious of ingratitude, she could not seem to free herself from a deep weariness of spirit, mind and body. Her doctor diagnosed a hernia, probably caused in part by too much heavy lifting. An operation was recommended. Alice felt strong guidance to go on a spiritual retreat for a week before deciding about the surgery. After a few days at the peaceful Retreat her entire being seemed to relax. She was filled with the Love of God—formerly quenched by that spirit of ingratitude in her heart—and *knew* that she was going to be healed. That night "the Peace that passeth understanding" came over her whole person. It seemed as if a slight movement of an "unseen hand" was repairing the inner physical need. She continued to pray daily with thanksgiving that this healing was being completed.

When she returned to her doctor, he suggested exercise and dieting to lose excess weight instead of an operation. She recognized that her desire for sweets had become a sin of gluttony, partly because her unhappy state of mind had been causing her to eat too much as compensation. When she prayed for Jesus to give her His self-control, the overwhelming desire for sweets was removed, along with her customary dislike of taking exercises. Thanking God for His healing Power at work within her, Alice dieted and exercised away the excess pounds before returning to her doctor. "Well," he said after examining the results of tests and X-rays, "if you want an operation, I can do it, but you really don't need it now!" She went on her way, rejoicing that the Lord had forgiven her gluttony and self-pity, restoring her to the joy of thanksgiving as He had miraculously repaired her body. If our bodily needs remind us of the greater need to overcome our corroding emotions, they can become stepping-stones to more complete health and a new dimension of life.

Guilt Feelings

Guilt feelings are deadly scorpions that seem to release a special venom to debilitate the one who secretly holds them. Edith was an active member of her Church, doing all sorts of good works and taking great care in the never-ending details of her five children's lives. In addition, she was burdened by some of her husband's real problems in a highly competitive business world and the possessive love of her mother who seemed to enjoy creating problems for Edith to solve. Her resentments began to build up toward her mother. But they were overlaid by guilt because of material assistance accepted from her mother without the response of genuine appreciation and love. Eventually Edith collapsed under the strain of trying to "play God to everyone in her family"—trying to be all things to all people. Her guilt feelings had mushroomed until she could not separate the true from the false. Her subconscious mind held such a confused set of "orders" that she became weak in spirit and body and distressed in mind, necessitating a complete withdrawal from life into the four walls of her home.

Fortunately, her husband's position required that they move to a distant city so that the direct problem with her mother was temporarily solved. The husband's understanding and the older children's helpfulness enabled her to have a "healing climate" of love in their new home. She met a neighbor who took a loving interest in her problems and gave her name to our prayer group, where she was faithfully prayed for by several "unknown friends-in-Christ". Months passed, and slowly Edith grew physically stronger, but she still remained unable to go out of her home to Church, to the prayer group or even to see friends. Daily meditating on the

Gospels and the Lord's healing Power had helped a little. But guilts continued to deprive her of much-needed peace of mind. When I went to see her, it was clear that healing could follow easily, if she would talk over these guilt feelings toward her mother. Together we asked God's forgiveness for some of them while releasing most which (on examination) proved to be false or exaggerated. I prayed for healing of old scars of earlier childhood difficulties which were still troubling her very sensitive spirit. Week by week, the Lord performed His miracle of dissolving these negative emotions in His Love. She began to lose the fear of meeting people and on Easter Day went to church with her family in the morning and for an outing that afternoon! Two months later she was a different person—gay, warm-hearted, praying for others even as she had been prayed for. When shortly afterwards news came that they must again move to another city, Edith *knew* that God had already prepared the right place for them. As each detail unfolded in perfect order, she continued to thank God for His healing Love empowering her to take up her life once more and meet new responsibilities victoriously. She was able to face each one in faith, *believing* in her heart: "I have strength for anything through him who gives me power" (Philippians 4:13).

It is evident that we, as individuals, are quite capable of setting up very effective "road blocks" on the highway to healing, but it is often too painful to remove these barriers alone! How much the emotionally distressed and physically ill need "listening posts" and prayer partners—God's servants (be they ministers or trusted Christian friends) who are not too busy to listen. Under the guidance of the Holy Spirit with prayer, patience and a more objective point of view, they can help the confused to sort out real from fantasy problems before it is too late. There is a ministry of the laity awaiting those who in faith and love will choose to be chosen by our Lord to serve Him in fulfilling this need. Ministers' wives, like Genevieve Parkhurst, often feel called into this ministry of listening. Through her talks on the healing of the memories at a CFO retreat, many found the courage to face old memories, "hidden in the basement of the house of life", to let the Love of Jesus purify the musty rooms. If we are trusting in Him to show us how and where, our Lord will bring those who need to experience His healing Love through us.

THE GIFTS OF THE SPIRIT

Thus far, we have looked at Divine Healing theologically as part of God's Will, historically in the ministry of Jesus, medically through the faith of Christian doctors, prayerfully through the intercession of the "priesthood of all believers" and sacramentally through the ministry of the Church. We have considered many sample case histories—those that taught me the most in my own personal healing adventure with Christ. Real-life stories have illustrated some of the major hindrances and helps to healing. What about the charismatic "gifts of healing" spoken of by St. Paul in I Corinthians 12:9, 30?

Charismatic gifts of healing appear to be given to certain individuals so that they can work more effectively as part of the Body of Christ. Often these gifts are received after the laying-on of hands or at times of individual prayer, but sometimes they are unsolicited by the person. In my own case I had not sought the Baptism in the Holy Spirit as such, because I had been taught that this experience was only for the Apostolic Age. The Lord had given me a prophecy that I was to go to Japan where I would teach some Bible classes and "help to start" a theological school. To my amazement, a few weeks later my husband received orders to duty in Japan! He flew out ahead, leaving us at home to wait for government housing to become available. In that year it seemed as if the Lord provided His equivalent of a theological training for me. Nevertheless, as I drove two thousand miles to the port of embarkation, I felt most inadequate. At last, safely aboard the transport, our two children set out to explore it. I knelt in our cabin alone. Suddenly I felt immersed in the Love of Jesus, as if I had been baptized with such overwhelming Love that I could only praise Him who had brought us safely through a long and hazardous journey to this oasis of peace! My heart filled with a rapturous joy such as I had never experienced before. I had been earnestly praying during all of the many months of waiting that the Lord would prepare me in any way He chose for whatever He planned for me to do, and suddenly I *knew* that He had answered that prayer in a most wonderful and unexpected way! It was as if at last I understood what St. Paul meant when he wrote: "The life I now live is not my life, but the life which Christ lives in me" (Galatians 2:20).

In the ensuing months things began to be done *through* me—things I could not possibly have done from my own resources. The teaching in a non-Christian Japanese woman's university developed into several areas far beyond my ability, yet fruit was obvious. My first book was written in a way so guided by the Lord that I still marvel. And the theological school was "started" that night in Tokyo, when the Dean of St. Paul's University came to dinner at our home and told us of his dream and the need on his campus! The first two students received their scholarships owing to the Lord's provision through us and our prayer group friends at home. Later the royalties from my first book went to this scholarship fund along with other gifts from home. And finally, a large donation came from the Dean's own American seminary. Thus I learned that Jesus could use even me to fulfill *His* purposes—as long as I was willing!

Let us consider what St. Paul wrote to the Corinthians: "Now there are varieties of gifts, but the same Spirit; and there are varieties of service, but the same Lord; and there are varieties of working, but it is the same God who inspires them all in every one. To each is given the manifestation of the Spirit for the common good" (I Corinthians 12:4-7, RSV). Then St. Paul described the nine gifts (or manifestations) as: "the utterance of wisdom . . . the utterance of knowledge . . . faith . . . gifts of healing . . . the working of miracles . . . prophecy . . . the ability to distinguish between spirits . . . various kinds of tongues . . . the interpretation of tongues" (12:8-10, RSV). After enumerating these charismatic gifts, he added firmly: "All these are inspired by one and the same Spirit, who apportions to each one individually as he wills" (12:11, RSV). In other words, the Holy Spirit will manifest Himself in these various ways "for the common good", i.e., for the building up of the Church, "the body of Christ".

After having described symbolically the interdependence of members of the Church by comparing them to parts of the body, St. Paul stated: "Now you are the body of Christ and individually members of it. And God has appointed in the church first apostles, second prophets, third teachers, then workers of miracles, then healers, helpers, administrators, speakers in various kinds of tongues" (12:27, 28, RSV). Recognizing that some people are given by God the special ability to channel His Healing Power just as others are called to be prophets or administrators, St. Paul closed his explanation of the gifts of the Spirit by saying, "earnestly desire the higher gifts" (12:31 RSV). Admittedly, his purpose in this section of the Epistle is stated in the first verse: "Now concerning spiritual gifts, brethren, I do not want you to be uninformed." To put it briefly, he was urging his Christian brothers in Corinth to seek these spiritual (higher) gifts needed for effective service in the Church. To carry on our Lord's supernatural ministry, His followers would need to be endowed with supernatural gifts!

At this point, St. Paul interrupted himself to remind the Corinthians that *none* of these "higher gifts" was of any real value *unless used in love*. He did *not* say that "love" is a "higher gift", but he insisted eloquently that *it is a "more excellent way"*. In my own case the gifts of wisdom, knowledge, faith, discernment and prophecy were needed for the accomplishment of the teaching and writing that the Lord had called me to do in Japan. But had the gifts not been used in the Way of Love, the work would have been ineffective.

To use the gifts of the Holy Spirit *without love* is. to debase or nullify their full value and effectiveness. There has been much misunderstanding about this point but a study of Scripture makes it clear that St. Paul considered "love" to be a *fruit* of the Spirit, not a gift (Galatians 5:22). The Corinthians badly needed this advice, for although they had many spiritual gifts, they were guilty of *mis*using them in spiritual pride rather than in patience, kindness, humility, unselfishness (all part of his basket of spiritual fruit). This is an equally serious danger for us today.

Having described the *Way of Love* as the greatest (faith and hope being runners-up, so to speak) St. Paul urged: "Make love your aim." And he repeated his earlier point: "earnestly desire the spiritual gifts" (14:1, RSV). He knew that without the supernatural gifts of the Holy Spirit, the Lord's work could not prosper to the fullest in view of the persecutions in store for the relatively small and weak (humanly speaking) communities of Christians. How much we need the gifts of wisdom, faith and discernment to *know how to pray today!*

Because the gifts of tongues, interpretation of tongues, and prophecy were being misunderstood and *mis*-used at Corinth, St. Paul then proceeded to concentrate most of his thought on these three gifts in order to correct abuses. He gave the Church what we might call today "Robert's Rules of Order" to govern the practice or use of these gifts *in public.* Wisely he warned Christians in Corinth: "God is not a God of confusion but of peace" (14:33 RSV). He summarized his admonitions in that last verse: "So, my brethren, earnestly desire to prophesy, and do not forbid speaking in tongues; but all things should be done decently and in order" (14:39, 40 RSV). St. Paul clarified his aims: "He who speaks in a tongue edifies himself, but he who prophesies edifies the church. Now I want you all to speak in tongues, but even more to prophesy. He who prophesies is greater than he who speaks in tongues, unless someone interprets, so that the church may be edified" (14:4, 5 RSV). Almost in the next breath he added: "Therefore, he who speaks in a tongue should pray for the power to interpret" (14:13 RSV).

St. Paul boasted that he himself prayed in a tongue, saying: "I thank God that I speak in tongues more than you all" (14:18 RSV). In fact, he said that in his private devotions he would "pray with the spirit and . . . with the mind also" (14:15 RSV). But his purpose in all this dissertation was to show that *in the public services of the Church* "I would rather speak five words with my mind, in order to instruct others, than ten thousand words in a tongue" (14:19, RSV). He concluded: "Let all things be done for edification" (14:26, RSV). His advice is still good for us today: " . . . since you are eager for manifestations of the Spirit, strive to excel in building up the church" (14:12, RSV). We need especially the gift of Wisdom to discern the Lord's Will—to do His work in His way and place and time—to build up *His* Church.

Gifts of healing should likewise be used for the building up of the Church, not for personal glorification but for the Lord's glory. The Church needs to draw into her ministry of the "priesthood of all believers" those having charismatic gifts of healing. In *Christian Healing,* Dr. Frost concludes: "When natural endowment and spiritual gift are both united to the service of redemptive love and the glory of God, then the individual will be especially fitted for the work of healing, even in the same way as when to the natural aptitude for teaching there is given also the corresponding spiritual *charisma,* thus rendering the individual peculiarly fitted for the teaching ministry within the body corporate."[1]

However, let us not lose sight of the fact that *the Gift of the Holy Spirit* is more important than *any* of the manifestations or gifts. Although the Book of Acts evidences the wide operation of *all* nine gifts listed by St. Paul, its main emphasis is not just on the gifts but rather on the Holy Spirit (the Gift) and Jesus (the Giver). The Holy Spirit is mentioned on over forty occasions.

Our Lord did not tell His disciples that they would have to go on without Him, powerless in the face of skepticism and real persecution. He promised: "I will ask the Father, and he will give you another to be your Advocate, who will be with you for ever—the Spirit of truth . . . he will bear witness to me . . . He will glorify me" (John 14:16, 17; 15:26; 16:14). The gifts are given for these purposes: to lead the believer into all Truth, to bear witness to Jesus and to glorify Him. Jesus admonished the disciples that they should wait in Jerusalem until they had received Power. Until they were baptized in the Holy Spirit at Pentecost, they were still timid men and women. But they were *obedient!*

In his splendid commentary, *The Acts of the Apostles,* Dr. William Barclay calls the Book of Acts the Gospel of the

Holy Spirit. Reminding us that the doctrine of the Holy Spirit is one we most need to re-emphasize today, he stresses the Early Church's obedience. So what about our glaring modern disobedience to our Lord's command to heal?

It has been said that young people drift away from the Church because to them Christianity seems irrelevant to modern life. They notice that the Church claims a power, but they feel we are hypocrites because they do not see that power at work in the world. In the Early Christian Church the non-Christians saw supernatural Power and Love manifested in the Christian community. We must know the reality of Christ living in us, if we are to witness to and "turn on the *now* Generation" in its unprecedented numerical strength. Convinced that we have failed, they are moving rapidly in the valley of disastrous decisions.

St. Luke made it quite clear that the early Church was filled with the Holy Spirit and with Power. There was no doubt in the minds of the first Christians that the Resurrection was *real;* that Jesus was a Living Presence in their midst; that they could call upon His Name to heal the sick; that He would be abiding in them always; that because they had truly received Him, they had been given the Power to become the sons of God. How many Christians so believe today? Dr. Barclay has called Jesus "the hinge of all history", for in becoming man He entered human life in such a way that it could never be as it was. For those first Christians (and for many today) life became an adventure with Christ, albeit a dangerous one. The disciples were so filled with His joy at Pentecost that they were accused of being "drunk with new wine"—and their joy sustained them, even in persecution. In Rome a few years ago as I viewed the Colosseum my spirit was deeply moved at the thought of Christians who sang hymns of joy as they were thrown to wild animals! Would we today?

St. Peter's first act after Pentecost was to preach a sermon that converted three thousand of his audience. The climax of it was: "repent and be baptized, every one of you, in the name of Jesus the Messiah for the forgiveness of your sins; and you will receive the gift of the Holy Spirit" (Acts 2:38). Although today the Church teaches that the Holy Spirit is given in baptism, few people seem to take this very seriously; they are more concerned with how the baby is dressed and whether it smiles or cries!

We are today, on the whole, too much like the people at Ephesus. When asked by St. Paul, "Did you receive the Holy Spirit when you became believers?" they replied: "No . . . we have not even heard that there is a Holy Spirit" (Acts 19:2, 3). Instead of arguing over whether or not "God is dead", we might do better to help our many troubled friends find for themselves His transforming Presence through personal experience. Divine Healing is one way to know His Love.

In speaking to the Gentile Cornelius, his relatives and close friends, St. Peter proclaimed the Good News, saying, "You know about Jesus of Nazareth, how God anointed him with the Holy Spirit and with power. He went about doing good and healing all who were oppressed by the devil, for God was with him. And we can bear witness to all that he did in the Jewish country-side and in Jerusalem" (Acts 10:38, 39).

If Jesus of Nazareth needed to be anointed by God with the Holy Spirit and with power, how much more do we today! The Bible does not mince words about the reality of Satan. St. Peter's first Epistle has the warning: "Awake! be on the alert! Your enemy the devil, like a roaring lion, prowls round looking for someone to devour. Stand up to him, firm in faith, and remember that your brother Christians are going through the same kinds of suffering while they are in the world" (5:8, 9).

In *World Aflame,* Dr. Billy Graham writes: "The Bible teaches that Satan can transform himself into an 'angel of light', adapting himself to every culture and every situation, even at times deceiving true believers. Counterfeiters always try to make their counterfeit money look exactly like the real thing. This is how Satan operates today. Thousands of people have been herded even into the church without a vital experience with Jesus Christ. They have substituted good works, community effort, social reform or a religious rite for personal salvation. Many people have just enough natural religion to make them immune to the real thing."[2]

We live in the Age of False Prophets which the Bible predicted. There are many in high theological positions who disagree over how much of the Scriptures are to be trusted as valid. In my university days the professor who debunked the miracles of Jesus helped to destroy my faith in God. If miracles were myths, what could I believe? If the Resurrection were only the disciples' subjective experience, then what was the validity of the Christian faith? If the words of Jesus were not true, then He was a Deceiver, not the Savior of the world. In trying to make the Christian faith palatable to intellectual skeptics, the professor destroyed its whole meaning. Many years and many bitter experiences later, I found the Living Christ in the healing of my young son; by the loving mercy of His Grace my childhood faith was once more restored!

One wonders whether or not modernism could have made such an impact if the Church had continued to practice its ministry of Divine Healing. Fortunately, there are Churches today where the Holy Spirit is truly worshipped as the Third Person of the Trinity—as God in action in the world today. When my husband's second heart attack forced us to seek a home in a milder climate, the Lord led us to such a Church. Here, where the gifts of the Spirit are operative and the fruit of Love, Joy and Peace are evident, people's lives are being changed. Skepticism dissolves before the redemptive Power of God. When one sees the transformed lives, the privilege of being His channel of healing Love far outweighs the long hours of patient prayer and listening. Through the lay ministry of our Church the Lord strengthens and extends the ministry of the priests. As the Body of Christ we hear our Lord's words once more: "And these signs will accompany those who believe: in my name they will cast out demons; they will speak in new tongues; they will pick up serpents, and if they drink any deadly thing, it will not hurt them; they will lay their hands on the sick, and they will recover" (Mark 16:17, 18, RSV).

When one has faced death and been healed by the Lord's gracious gift of health, no arguments are needed to convince him that Christ lives today. He does not need to be cajoled into minimum giving; he is more apt to tithe. When one commits his life to follow Christ he soon finds that, if he is truly in earnest about this, he needs—and receives—far more than his natural aptitudes and powers can supply. When a modern disciple has received the Baptism in the Holy Spirit, the Love and Peace and Joy bestowed by the Lord Jesus bear witness to His glory, not to man's rationalizations. We are given the words to witness and the Power to live so that not we but the Lord will be glorified. We are not promised a bed of roses—but we *are* empowered to bear our part of our Lord's Cross!

One of the healthiest signs in our churches today is the return to "New Testament Christianity", where lay people witness to what Christ has done in their lives. In my own experience, when Satan has tempted me to doubt, the *reality* of that first Divine Healing of my child has been my best defence. When we have experienced Christ's healing touch in our lives, we *know Him,* because we have been "ransomed, healed, restored, forgiven".

In Faith-at-Work conferences and Lay Witness or Faith Alive Missions, committed Christians of all denominations share their witness with those who (though members of Churches) have not as yet found for themselves a vital confrontation with the living Christ. Recently, at such a gathering, a man came into the seminar I was leading on "Healing and Wholeness". A Christian who visited him in hospital had prayed for healing of the pain which had seriously crippled him for many years. She had persuaded him and his wife to come at once to this conference. When he heard another man's witness, our new friend realized the full meaning of the healing he had received but was in danger of losing! In amazement he said, "But every word you spoke was just for me!" Then falteringly he began to tell the group of his illness and of the Christian woman who had prayed with such confidence in the Lord's power to heal. While he witnessed, his pallid face began to glow and he gave thanks publicly to the Lord. He was being healed as he shared this experience with us. That night he played the piano as his wife sang to the glory of God. Many who saw him had to look twice to recognize him as the man who had come to our group meeting a few hours before.

The world needs renewal of the laity in *every* walk of life. We belong to "the priesthood of all believers". God works through those who have real, living faith in Him. I know of no greater adventure than committing one's life to Jesus, the Healing Christ, to be used by Him as He chooses to release His healing Power into the world that is sick unto death with hate and fear. Only the supernatural gifts of the Holy Spirit can prevail against forces of evil infiltrating even in high places.

THE DELIVERANCE MINISTRY

We live in a troubled world with wars and rumors of wars, mounting divorce rates and increased mental illness. We are torn by riots and slum tensions in a wilderness of political cross claims. Our problems of new morality and youth burden the hearts of not only parents but also even would-be parents. The new theology confuses those who believe fervently that God *is*—regardless of man's unbelief—and that He cannot be whittled down to man's size! There are devastating forces of hate, fear and guilt unleashed in human hearts. What is wrong with the human race today? Where is the Church's healing Power coping with the needs?

We as the Body of Christ are sickly compared to the dynamic members of the Early Christian Church. Our obedience, our commitment and consequently our faith and witness have seriously diminished. Man's need is just as great, and the Gospel is still as relevant as ever. But the farce is that we are trying, as the Reverend Archer Torrey says, to "be relevant without the Relator, the Holy Spirit".

In the stress of modern life, the Church cannot expect to achieve the desired impact on human need unless our Master's express commands are followed: "As you go, proclaim the message: 'The kingdom of Heaven is upon you.' Heal the sick, raise the dead, cleanse lepers, cast out devils. You received without cost; give without charge" (Matthew 10:7,8). This commission to the Twelve Apostles as they started on their missionary journeys (Luke 9:1-6) was similarly repeated to the seventy-two others (Luke 10:1-12), and they returned jubilantly, saying that even the devils had responded to their commands (Luke 10:17-20). During the last days of His earthly ministry, Jesus commissioned the eleven apostles (and us through them) to observe all that He had commanded. He assured them that He would be with them even to the end of time (Matthew 28:18-20). In St. Mark's Gospel the specific promise was given: "Faith will bring with it these miracles: believers will cast out devils in my name and speak in strange tongues; . . . and the sick on whom they lay their hands will recover" (16:17-18).

In Scandinavia, a nurse who had been healed by the Lord at our Ashram Retreat made such a joyous impression on two traveling companions that they were converted before the journey's end. Instead of making a compelling impact on the pagans around us by the vitality of our Christian fellowship, all too often the Church is scarcely different from equally well-meaning secular institutions. "Behold these Christians, how they love one another!" is seldom exclaimed of our Churches today as it was in the earliest days. Indeed, for the most part, the Church has attempted to evangelize without the Gospel proclamation of Divine Healing, as if our higher civilization rendered impossible a vital faith in the Healing Christ today. But where the Divine Commission is being carried out in faith, we have found that an impelling vitality has come into the Church.

In England, in 1944, the Churches' Council of Healing stated that Church members can be instruments of God's healing Power as they offer themselves in a ministry of intercessory prayer. This is simply a restatement of the faith of the Church during the first five centuries before the idea crept into the liturgies and prayers that sickness was a "divine chastisement". As we have seen, the Primitive Church rallied to fight against sickness as a clear violation of the Will of God. Those who were sick were considered to be victims (a) of their own sin; (b) of the "sin of the world" (of man's disobedience against God); or (c) of Satanic bindings. But whether or not sin was personal or corporate, it was the task of the Church to manifest the power of the Healing Christ by the prayer of faith. It was also the task of the Church to exorcise those who were victims of evil spirits. In fact, exorcism preceded baptism in the Early Christian Church.

Apparently many modern Christians think of Satan as a myth. Yet how else can we explain the many horrible things that are happening in our times? How much of the terrible increase in mental illness today can be attributed to some evil force—call it what you will—that seems to possess and twist personalities? An increasing number commit dreadful crimes against their fellow men. Senseless assassinations result from the violent hates, jealousies and fears of emotionally unstable persons in all walks of life.

We read in the newspapers of people believing in reincarnation. There is a marked increase of dangerous preoccupation with the occult, the psychic level, contrary to Biblical teaching. Mind-bending drugs (LSD), marijuana, alcoholism and glue-sniffing are thought by some to be "escapes from reality", but in fact they are dead-end streets! The only reality they lead to is bondage to forces of evil. Only the Power of Jesus can deliver those who in ignorance or curiosity or willful disobedience to Scripture put themselves at Satan's mercy.

In his newspaper column, *My Answer,* Dr. Billy Graham once wrote that he could prove the devil's reality by the tragic results of his fiendish handiwork in the world about us. To a questioner who sought to explain away the devil as the evil within man's heart, Dr. Graham replied that Christ (who was Himself without sin) was tempted three times. The evangelist then warned the man to beware of Satan who as a personality was lying in wait to trap him and others like him who were not on guard against his demonic wiles.

The assaults of Satan were very real to Jesus in the wilderness and to His followers, the "saints" of the early Christian Church. We later-day Christians sing hymns about the Church being "like a mighty army". In our baptismal vows, we promise "to renounce the devil and all his works, the vain pomp and glory of the world, with all covetous desires of the same, and the sinful desires of the flesh."[1] The minister then prays that the person being baptized "may have power and strength to have victory, and to triumph, against the devil, the world, and the flesh".[2] Are these just meaningless words we are mouthing, or do we really take our baptismal vows seriously? Do we even bother to identify Satan and call on Jesus for protection? A young Marine officer who became an Episcopal priest once ruefully said:

"I'm still in the service, but it's a Higher Service. The trouble is that the troops are more undisciplined, and the air cover (prayer power) is weaker, and the Enemy is more subtle!" In the Bible, Satan is called "the great deceiver", "the prince of this world" and "the father of lies."

There are times when one feels that although God brings good out of evil, His highest Will has not been done. Because He did not make man as a puppet, evil is permitted to exist where man chooses to misuse his God-given freedom of will and disobey God's Plan. *God chose to limit Himself when He delegated to man freedom of will.* Many things are part of God's circumstantial or permissive Will but not His intentional Will.

In the case, for example, of a drunkard who drives his car into an innocent bystander, killing the father of a family of young children, we can see that Satan lured the driver from one "innocent drink" to a state of intoxication. We see here that the "sin of the world" is clearly an impediment to God's perfect Will for this family—surely this was not His intentional Will! If the persons involved surrender their wills to God, He can bring good even out of such evil. In one such incident the offender was converted by the truly Christian forgiveness of the bereaved family, and the grace of God strengthened the mother and children, drawing them into closer communion with Himself. As they radiated God's Peace, their needs were provided for through His Love and the compassion of others. Although man's sinful folly and Satan's temptations prevailed to cause the accident, when the situation was lifted to God, blessings came from it on an almost unbelievable scale.

On the other hand, if the injured persons should become bitter instead of trusting God to bring forth good, His healing power would be limited by misuse of their God-given freedom of will. The drunken driver, burdened by guilt, could easily become a confirmed alcoholic. The embittered mother would add a spiritual warping to the loss which she and the children already bore. Sooner or later physical illness would very likely result. Through her resentment and self-pity, Satan could block the "healing" that God yearned to bring out of the situation created by the sin of drunken driving (abuse of God-given freedom of will). In such a case the prayers of a "believing community" could be God's channels to allow His Love to deliver the hearts of all concerned from their burdens and bondage—to bring Divine Healing. To try to comfort this mother and her bereaved children by telling them that such a tragedy was the intentional and purposeful Will of God would ultimately result in their resentment of God (either outwardly or secretly). It is more true to admit that although Satan had his way, our Lord has promised His deliverance for those who accept His Grace: He bears our burdens and heartaches with us.

Healing of the Scars of the Past

Someone has well said, "God will not look you over for medals, degrees or diplomas, but for scars." Unfortunately, sometimes the old scars of past hurts are very real and deep in the subconscious mind. Although the patient may not have strong faith, if she will but fix her eyes on Jesus and His Love, the faith of the one praying for the healing of these wounds can be used to channel His Love backward in time to touch, cleanse and heal painful recollections and thoughts that are still binding the unhappy person. The person who prays thus must *know* that the power of the Resurrection is available today when claimed by faith. Jesus often used the faith of another to bring healing to the one in need. Jesus is the same—yesterday, today and forever—so that He can easily go backward in time to find the grieving person (or more often the hurt child) who still "lives in the subconscious" mind of the grown person. We have only to *believe* that the power He released on the Cross is effective today to heal and to bless—and then claim *His* victory in expectant faith!

Because there are an increasing number of people counterfeiting this scripturally valid ministry, it is important to insist on the deep prayer counseling done under the auspices of Victorious Ministry Through Christ.* In such lengthy appointments, the counselee experiences the Power of the Name of

---

* This is the name of the religious, educational organization which was incorporated to support our Clergy Schools of Prayer Counselling. All royalties, book profits, and "love offerings" received by the author go into this fund. Schools are held in various parts of the U.S.A., in England and Sweden.

Jesus and the Blood shed on Calvary: to break unnatural dependencies and bondages (Lev. 20:26); to bind and cast out oppressing or possessing spirits (Acts 10:38); and to forgive sins (James 5:15b-16; I John 1:8-9). After acceptance of salvation (Acts 16:31; St. John 1:12) the person who has been set free by the Lord is ready to receive the Baptism (or a fresh infilling) of the Holy Spirit as promised in Luke 11:13 and the claiming of gifts (I Cor. 12:7-11) and fruit (Gal. 5:22-23). The purpose of this deep prayer counseling is to lead the counselee out of all bondages (no matter how long or with whom they have existed) into total commitment to the Lord. Only then is this person free to forget the past and "press on toward the goal for the prize of the upward call of God in Christ Jesus" (Phil. 3:14). Because of the prevalence of alcoholic, drug and other addictions and the oppression of occult spirits, a large part of the lengthy appointment is spent in teaching on repentance, deliverance and commitment. Those interested in deeper knowledge of the dangers of dabbling in the many prevalent forms of the occult are referred to *The Holy Spirit and You* by Dennis and Rita Bennett[3] and *Spiritual Warfare* by Michael Harper.[4] Many passages of Scripture (both Old and New Testament) forbid occult practices: we have been warned by God and we disobey at our own peril!

At a Christian healing home in England, I met a woman who was suffering from a serious heart condition that had left her a semi-invalid. Fearful because of this illness and resentful because of her broken marriage, Sheila was a most unhappy, unhealthy person. One evening we went to the chapel and prayed for her bitter memories of the past to be healed. We claimed that the Light of Christ would go backward in time to identify and heal by enfolding in His Love the moments of grief, shock, anger, self-pity and depression that lay buried in her subconscious mind. With real penitence she asked God to forgive her sins of anger and bitterness toward her divorced husband who in deserting her many years before had left her to bring up two daughters alone. Then she asked Jesus to give her a real spirit of "forgiving-ness" toward this one who had so deeply hurt her. A wonderful Peace filled the small chapel—the Peace that passes understanding. That night Sheila had a beautiful and unexpected experience of the Love of Christ in a vision, and assurance of His healing power. Two weeks later, when she began her arduous journey home, we met in London, and I rejoiced with her that she was truly a new person in Christ Jesus. The Lord provided quite miraculously for her needs, and she arrived home full of joy and faith, a very different woman from the one who had left two weeks before. Her daughters, her vicar and her friends marveled at the change which continued until she was restored to perfect health. Within two years she was offering her services in loving gratitude in another healing home nearer her city. She witnessed to God's glory, not only with her voice but also in her life of consecrated service to others. To Sheila, it has been a resurrection experience, because for years she had thought that life had passed her by.

Dr. Hans Selye, the Canadian research physiologist, has studied the effect of stress on the body's hormone production. The pituitary and adrenal glands release excess hormones in times of emotional or physical strain to meet the body's needs. However, if this is a chronic response, the overworking of these glands can lead to lowered resistance to disease. According to reports on Dr. Selye's experiments, the condition can be a significant factor in causing heart disease, hypertension, rheumatic fever and arthritis. Obviously, the deeper the person's consciousness of God, the more His Peace can counteract the emotional and physical stresses and strains of life.

Exorcism

A divorcee with four children was about to reject and abandon them. Fortunately, a friend, knowing that Carolyn was really running from her responsibilities, urged her to come to our Church for counselling. My rector and I prayed for her to be set free from the bondage to a "spirit of rejection" which had plagued her since early childhood. By faith in the protection of the Blessed Trinity over all spirits contrary to the Holy Spirit and in the Name of Jesus, calling upon the power of His precious Blood, we exorcised this spirit. As it left her she showed visible signs of release from inner pressure. Next we bound and exorcised a "spirit of fear", claiming the power of the perfect Love of Jesus to cast out fear. Since there is no condemnation in Christ Jesus, we bound and cast out in His Name the "spirit of self-condemnation". Next we felt guided to bind and cast out a "spirit of anxiety" about her future, reminding her that Jesus said, "Do not be anxious about tomorrow." By this time she was able to face her "spirit of resentment" against the husband who had divorced her to marry another woman. Again, by the Power of the Blood of Jesus that was shed for .her deliverance, we exorcised this deeply buried spirit. She wept copiously but appeared greatly relieved, although quite empty and weak. It was time to pray for the infilling of the Holy Spirit—for her to be immersed in the Love of Jesus. She received the Baptism in the Holy Spirit for power to minister to her young family—to go on alone with Him. We prayed with great joy for Carolyn to be so filled with the Holy Spirit that all the fruit might be borne in her life: peace that passes understanding; love that can love the unlovable; joy that does not depend on circumstances; patience with her children and with herself; kindness, goodness, gentleness; faithfulness to the promises of Jesus; humility to accept all that He wanted to bring forth in her life. We prayed that she might live under the control of the Holy Spirit, not under the domination of her own will power or the dominion of other people's wills.

At last we prayed for the supernatural gifts of the Holy Spirit, knowing that she would need them to bring up her four children alone: wisdom to know God's Will in all things; knowledge of Jesus as her living Savior; discernment to make the right choices for herself and her children—to discern evil from good; faith to believe that in her weakness the strength of Jesus would be perfected. In accordance with Ephesians 6:10-18, we prayed for Jesus to put on her the whole armor of God: the helmet of salvation (the knowledge of His saving Grace); the breast-plate of righteousness (His righteousness, not her own, so that her life might show right-useness); the girdle of truth that she might know His Truth and be set free to walk in His Way, His Resurrected Life abiding within her; and the shoes of the gospel of peace, that He might guide her feet through each doorway, closing the wrong ones and opening the right ones, preparing the way for her. We prayed for the shield of faith that it might envelop Carolyn like a great tent, protecting her from faithless fears; and for the sword of the Spirit, the Living Word of God, that it might well up within her, cutting her free from any false bondages so that she might be bound only to Jesus, now and into all eternity. Then she knelt and committed her life to Him "whose service is perfect freedom" in thanksgiving for His deliverance. With a deep sense of peace, an undercurrent of joy, a visible radiation of His Love in her eyes, she went forth from the church to take up her family responsibilities in the awareness of the Love and Power of Jesus who would guide and sustain her as she gazed on Him and not on the wreckage of her life. Only the Lord Jesus could win such a victory in a few short hours!

With Gloria, another young married woman, it was necessary by faith to take "the sword of the Spirit" and cut the bondages to her very possessive parents and also to her domineering husband, so that she could be freed from the tug-of-war going on among them. Some months before this, to satisfy her husband, she had broken contact with her parents, but her own guilts, fears, resentments and self-pity were all bound up with the overly-dominated child of the past who was still very much alive within the grown woman. We prayed for Jesus to cut these spiritual strings that were literally "tieing her up in knots". We prayed for the healing of relationships so that she could be free to love each of these three persons without putting herself under the domination of any of them.

Our Lord said that no man could serve two masters—and yet Gloria had been trying to serve all three with their conflicting demands upon her personality. It was no wonder that she had not been able to love any of them, that she and her husband had been legally separated for several months and that she had bitterly resented his and her parents' possessive love. Then, in the Name of Jesus and by the power He released on the Cross through the shedding of His Blood, we cast out, one by one, the spirits of rejection, fear, tension, anger, self-condemnation and self-pity. When each spirit left her, she coughed as if she would choke. After this "spiritual operation", she was amazed at how relieved she felt for the terrible, suffocating inner pressure was gone.

Then as I prayed for the healing of these wounds she was

released from the bondage of the "inner child" who had suffered many traumatic experiences buried both consciously and unconsciously. But they were still conditioning the grown woman to react, not on the basis of the present, but because of associations with her painful memories of the past. The Love of Jesus was prayed over them with thanksgiving that He was now cleansing and enfolding these old aching hurts with the healing power of His Love. It was as if they dissolved and there was no longer any pain associated with them. The forgiving Love of Jesus erased the chalk-marks of self-condemnation from the spiritual slate Gloria had carried in her heart; and her sense of guilt turned into gratitude to the Saviour who had thus delivered her from the bondage of the past.

As I continued to pray for the Love of Jesus to fill every cell, nerve, tissue and fibre of her being, she was able to realize and release many other memories that previously she had never been able to face alone because the pain of former rejection was too great. The spiritual therapy of His Love is powerful, for Jesus is the great Psychiatrist. He is the same yesterday, today and forever, so He can go back into the yesterdays and heal past buried experiences. The adult is thus set free to be the person God created her to be! *The one who so prays must have the faith to believe for the broken victim* in need of deliverance from the assaults of Satan and the sin of the world. Such a ministry of deliverance can not be undertaken lightly. It carries with it the great responsibility of personal surrender of intellect, spirit, will and body to the Holy Spirit.

At a recent retreat where I had been a prayer counsellor the Lord used me for the deliverance of many persons from bondage to their traumatic pasts. Three had come from the same Church. On the last morning their pastor, a Presbyterian, came to me asking what I was doing. "I've had a great deal of psychological counselling training and experience and I've worked with them for a year," he said, "but you work with them for two hours, and they are healed!" Of course, I immediately assured him that it was not I—it was the Lord. And that, as a Spirit-filled Christian, I was praying only as He had taught me to pray for those who had been victims of terrible experiences in their earlier years. In the "spiritual hot-house" of a retreat, the planted seed of healing grows more quickly. But the fruit that he had seen would continue to mature as the Presence of Jesus continued to deepen within the nurturing fellowship of their own Presbyterian church.

Keeping high the spirit of love and unity in the fellowship which welds us together as individuals, clergy and laity make up the Body of Christ who "ever lives to make intercession for us". Until the *whole* Church is convinced that the "prayer of faith" is God's instrument for saving the distressed—rather than the prayer of doubt, conditioned as man's mind is by the phrase *"If* it be Thy will"—the *fullness* of God's Grace can not be experienced.

To be effective, the gift of grace demands the response of the recipient. This, we might add, is as true of receiving healing, forgiveness and deliverance as it is of receiving the power for living. Grace does not displace or supersede our human will, intelligence or personality; it takes the human qualities of the person and makes them operative on a higher level so that the personality is integrated, freed from its destructive conflicts of will and oriented towards God's true purposes. In His Will is our Peace!

The claim that Apostolic healings were only for that particular age is now being disproved where the Church is trying to minister on a higher plane than Jumble sales, bazaars and art clubs. Although some people are drawn to the Church by such measures, spiritual revival has not been conspicuously present through these media. On the other hand, evangelism leading to conversion is one of the accompaniments of the healing ministry.

How greatly we need the *whole* Gospel, not just a personal or social Gospel, but a united front against the inroads of heathenism which are encouraged by the divided witness, spiritual ineffectiveness, and lack of love among us. Although we call ourselves Christians, we too often fail to claim the saving Power of our Lord and Master to deliver us from the very real assaults of Satan! Our Lord Himself *calls us* and uses us to be His "prayer warriors" in the battle of Life, so that the victory He won on the Cross almost two thousand years ago can become effective in the world today!

The spiritual conflict between good and evil is just as real now as when Christ was present in the flesh. A substantial amount of experience in exorcism was a characteristic of the Early Christian Church, and this is being proved valid by those who have the call and the courage to claim the Power of the Blood of Jesus over Satan's attacks today. When one holds fear or bitterness, hate or self-pity for an abnormal period of time, one allows the Enemy to possess the heart and mind that should be filled with the Love of Jesus. It is the work of the Holy Spirit to deliver that person from bondage through the channels offering themselves for this ministry of the Church. But the greatest battle is not in any earthly sphere, important as this may be. The ultimate decision is and always will be: "When Jesus returns, will He find faith on this earth?"

HEALING OF THE BODY OF CHRIST

This is the great healing work of the Church: to bring man into a state of union with God and with his fellow men through worship, study, witnessing, prayer, fellowship, service and commitment. The Body of Christ, the Church, is to proclaim the Good News of the unconditional Love of God, as available to the repentant Prodigal as to the most devout member in its pews. Its purpose as a Samaritan Church is to serve the world that has been "turned off" and lacks the relevance of healing prayer in its agonizing needs. The healing of the individual is a necessary part of the healing of the universal Body.

The Reformation (although it corrected many evils) gave birth to a new one: divisiveness. The purpose of the Ecumenical Movement is the healing of divisions within Christianity—healing of the Body of Christ, mutilated as it has been by schisms and controversies. We can thank God that ours is the Age of Integration in the divided Church, and our Lord's High Priestly prayer that we "all might be one" is now being considered seriously. Even a decade ago wise people would have laughed at a prophecy concerning the degree of re-union that has already begun to take place in the Universal Church; but let us pray that there is more healing yet to come. I am speaking of spiritual unity of *all* believers, praying and ministering together, not just organizational mergers to build bigger denominations.

My good friend the Reverend F. Noel Palmer writes in *The Pattern of Life:* "The Holy Spirit, by his presiding Presence in the Church, makes it the Body of Christ in life and reality, not merely in labels and outward form. Too often we think, talk, and act as if He were not really here, not actively in us;

and of course He is *not* in us, if we have not received Christ as Savior."[1] Not what denomination are you—but rather, have you committed your life to Jesus Christ as Savior? Did you receive the Holy Spirit? These are questions we need to ask if we are to find at the "grass-roots level" the *real* unity of the Body of Christ—real healing of our many divisions in Christendom.

We need to acknowledge the working of the Holy Spirit in all who put their trust in Christ (irrespective of their denominational labels) in order to find the true *koinonia,* or fellowship of agape Love. If Jesus is really our common denominator, we need not be so concerned over ecclesiastical, ritual differences. Instead of letting prejudice lead us away from each other, we who call ourselves by the Name of Christ can find true communion with Him and with each other when we are led by His Holy Spirit, the third Person of the Godhead.

In America, there are many denominations and sects of Christianity, all claiming to be the Truth. The Established Church in England is Anglican; in Scotland and Wales, Presbyterian; in Scandinavia, Lutheran; in Italy and France, Roman Catholic; in Greece, Greek Orthodox. How confusing this is to pagans in these countries and to the "heathen" in countries where Christianity can claim only a small percentage of their populations' religious belief! Which one of many claims and creeds should they believe? More likely, they will reject Christ and His proffered Love, because they fail to see His Love operating in those who call themselves Christians ("Christ-folk").

While doing some missionary teaching in a Japanese non-Christian University, I asked my students to memorize St. Paul's wonderful dissertation on Love (I Corinthians 13). It became obvious that they questioned after this: (a) why we could not agree on "the Truth"; (b) why we could not love those of other denominations; (c) why we had racial problems if we were all Christians!

We are engaged today in a huge ideological struggle between the forces of materialism and the life of the Spirit—between Communism and Christianity. Where there is divisiveness in either side, the other gains advantage. For survival, it behooves us to seek reconciliation with our "Christian brothers". Only the Holy Spirit can bring unity within diversity. Jesus promised that He would send His Spirit to indwell us and enable us to love one another because He first loved us enough to give His life's blood for us. Jesus was born into our earthly life to die for our salvation, beginning now and continuing into eternity.

In Heaven we shall be one. Surely there are no "reserved pews" there for Lutherans, Episcopalians, Presbyterians, Methodists, Pentecostals, Baptists or Roman Catholics! Nor is there a color bar! Surely there will be no division of yellow or black, or red or white; no segregation of national backgrounds, no special corners or corridors for Italians, Poles, Irish, English, Chinese or Americans! How can we expect to shed these racial and national controversies there if we do not at least make a prayerfully sincere attempt to solve them here? If we become one in Christ Jesus who loves *all* men, shall we not need to become reconciled with each other? Granted, this is easier in theology than in practice, and to accomplish it may take much time and prayer. Sin is our separation from God, and separation from each other truly separates us from God. In John's first Epistle, we read: "And indeed this command comes to us from Christ himself: that he who loves God must also love his brother" (4:21).

Only the working of the Cross in our lives here can change our pre-judging of people because of their way of worship, color or nationality. Only the working of Christ's Holy Spirit can replace our prejudices with His Love that wills *equally* the highest good for each human soul, regardless of denominational, racial or national labels. The healing of the Body of Christ can come only as we realize that Christ died for all races, all nations of men.

I first discerned the Body of Christ in this sense when I went to the service of consecration of a Japanese bishop. The words were Japanese of which I knew only a few, but they served to link me with those praying. As the service flowed on, my spirit was united with that gathering of Christian people of many nationalities, for Yokohama is quite an international seaport. Bishops and priests, merchants, diplomats and simple people gathered to pray for the Holy

Spirit to consecrate a fellow man who had been called by God to this ministry. The union of spirit transcended language barriers and racial and economic differences. We were all one in prayer, in praise and thanksgiving—to our Lord.

St. Paul's words to the Corinthians need to be heeded by us today: "For every time you eat this bread and drink the cup, you proclaim the death of the Lord, until he comes. It follows that anyone who eats the bread or drinks the cup of the Lord unworthily will be guilty of desecrating the body and blood of the Lord" (I Cor. 11:27-28). The divisions and separations among those who follow Christ affect the unity of His Body—which is not only in the consecrated elements of bread and wine at Holy Communion but also in the company of believers gathered together in His Name. Where there is not a climate of love, there is disobedience to the Lord's commands; there can be no real wholeness.

St. Paul cautioned the Christians at Corinth who had debased the sacred meaning of Communion: "A man must test himself before eating his share of the bread and drinking from the cup. For he who eats and drinks, eats and drinks judgement on himself if he does not discern the Body. That is why many of you are feeble and sick, and a number have died" (I Corinthians 11:28-30).

Are we rejecting our Lord's healing power when we fail to discern His Body and Blood today? Do we (like the people of Corinth) take too casually this tremendous privilege and *go unprepared in our hearts to receive the Lord of Life?*

At a healing service in England, I saw a woman whose face glowed with the radiant, unmistakable "healed look". Yes, it was true that she had been healed of incurable cancer after surgery had apparently failed. It was a slow healing, she said, that came as she discerned the Body and Blood of our Lord Jesus Christ. In those long bed-ridden days she had taken Holy Communion, believing that, in receiving the elements, she was really receiving the Body and Blood of the Savior who had all power by this infusing of His Perfect Life to heal the imperfection and *dis*-ease in her body. Daily she had meditated on this thought of the Living Bread. She had felt this transfusion of His precious Blood, His Resurrected Life taking place within her cells and tissues, as well as her spirit and mind. She had taken Jesus at His word, *nothing doubting,* clinging not to fear or self-pity but to the promise in Romans: "Moreover, if the Spirit of him who raised Jesus from the dead dwells within you, then the God who raised Christ Jesus from the dead will also give new life to your mortal bodies through his indwelling Spirit" (8:11). Her whole life was changed! And in the new life our blessed Lord had given her as a healed member of His Body the Church, she was now visiting the sick, interceding for others and even editing a healing magazine.

We must recall our Lord's own words the day after the feeding of the five thousand. When people had followed Him to Capernaum and questioned Him about His meaning of the "the real bread from heaven", Jesus said: "I am the bread of life . . . I am that living bread which has come down from heaven: if anyone eats this bread, he shall live for ever. Moreover, the bread which I will give is my own flesh; I give it for the life of the world . . . In truth, in very truth I tell you, unless you eat the flesh of the Son of Man and drink his blood you can have no life in you. Whoever eats my flesh and drinks my blood possesses eternal life, and I will raise him up on the last day" (John 6:48, 51, 53, 54). Are we today like the Jews who disputed fiercely, saying: "How can this man give us his flesh to eat? . . . This is more than we can stomach! Why listen to such words?" (John 6:52, 60). Shall we, like many of His disciples, withdraw because we cannot accept His teaching? Or shall we like Peter reply, "Lord, to whom shall we go? Your words are words of eternal life. We have faith, and we know that you are the Holy One of God" (John 6:68, 69).

In *The Power of the Blood,* Andrew Murray says that we drink in a person's words when we take them to heart, listening intently and accepting their truth. Although the Power of the Blood is a mystery to us, we can "drink His Blood" as we appropriate and use in our inner lives all that we do understand of its life-transforming quality. By *faith* we receive Power to appropriate our Lord's victory on the Cross over the evil forces in the world. We do not understand fully the mysteries of electricity, but we have faith in its power so that we use it.

Where can we better expose ourselves to the healing power of the Love of Jesus? We so often shut ourselves off from His Grace by running away in much busyness instead of turning to Him who alone has provided the means of changing us. A well-known professor urged young seminarians to go to the altar even if their hearts carried burdens of resentment — as long as their intention and desire was to be healed of them. To offer one's sins is as important as to offer one's talents. Until we try it, we cannot know how powerful is *reconciliation* through faith in the Blood of Jesus, our Savior. This was the purpose of His self-sacrifice. Deliverance from sin comes not by staying away from Communion but by true preparation and repentant acceptance, not by rationalizing, but by truly and humbly submitting ourselves to His Grace.

"If we walk in the light as he himself is in the light, then we share together a common life, and we are being cleansed from every sin by the blood of Jesus his Son" (I John 1:7). We need a Savior; we cannot save ourselves when faced with the demands of the Commandment to *love* all men as our neighbors. Once when I could not love a person in my own human love, I found it best to admit honestly to God what He already knew (my own lovelessness) and claim the power of Jesus to love this person *through* me. Much to my surprise, my whole attitude changed.

Because Jesus knew that we could never love in our own self-centeredness, He died — to give us the Pattern and the Power of His Life. Resurrection in Him comes through death of our own desires, wills and prejudices as we go *through* the Cross and claim the transforming Power of His precious Blood — *a spiritual transfusion* which alone saves our lives from cancers of hate, pride, fear and self-will. We must die to hate; we must die to pride; we must die to fear; we must die to self-will — to be born again! Without appropriating the cleansing Power of the Blood of Jesus the Christ, we are sure to fall short or fail.

Perhaps this is why we do so often fail. We do not appropriate this Power of the Blood because of our squeamishness. Yet we often say: "This group needs 'new blood'." We are quite willing to go to Holy Communion, but often we do not even consciously accept the words that we hear with our outward ears: "Almighty and everliving God, we most heartily thank Thee, for that Thou dost vouchsafe to feed us who have duly received these holy mysteries, with *the spiritual food of the most precious Body and Blood of Thy Son our Savior Jesus Christ*"[2] (italics mine).

Do we consciously leave the altar rail or Communion table with the joy of knowing that we have *really* just received this precious feeding of our spirits: that the Blood of Jesus, His Life-giving Spirit, has just cleansed us of all sin and the Spiritual Substance of His Body has just renewed and refreshed our spirits? Or is this just a memorial service? Do we really unite our hearts and intentions with those of the celebrant in this prayer? Or do the words just roll past our spiritual ears without impact? "Grant us therefore, gracious Lord, *so to eat the flesh of Thy dear Son Jesus Christ, and to drink his blood, that our sinful bodies may be made clean by his body, and our souls washed through his most precious blood,* and that we may evermore *dwell in him, and he in us*"[3] (italics mine).

Do we recognize the life-giving power of His Blood when we plead it for ourselves and others? And do we really believe that, as the Head of the human race, "The new Adam", our Blessed Lord, took *our* sins upon Himself: that with His own Life's Blood He paid in advance the price of *our* sins, so that we could face Holy God? By His death He paid for you the premium on this most precious insurance policy but you must sign on the dotted line of acceptance — real commitment — if it is to be effective in your own life. As you commit your life to Jesus, you receive far more from Him!

The committed life is one that begins with prayer and remains in tune with God throughout each day through listening prayer and flash prayers. Real communion with God is *dialogue* not monologue! We need to appropriate His grace. The Power that Jesus made available on the Cross must become a concrete reality by faith—personally accepted!

Without this, God's justice would require that you and I be eternally excluded from the Holiness that is His Presence. We do not expect an audience with a King or President unless someone paves the way. How much less are we worthy to stand in the Holiest of Holies, the Presence of Almighty God;

except that by becoming Man, Jesus paved the way for us! We are in ourselves entirely unworthy. In the Communion service we pray: "We are unworthy so much as to gather up the crumbs under thy Table. But thou art the same Lord, whose property is always to have mercy."[4] Do we really mean it? Having received His Presence through the sacrament we thank God that we are members of "the mystical body of Thy Son, which is blessed company of all faithful people . . ."[5]

Believers are still effective channels of God's healing power as St. James proclaimed them to be. The promises of Jesus about the two in agreement and the two or three met together in His Name are still valid. His Presence calls forth the prayer in His Nature of Love that is honored by our Heavenly Father; and the condition of agreement of two or more persons simply widens the channel for Him to use. Many have found that two praying in perfect agreement were a more usable channel for God's Power than two praying separately, although He uses "lone intercessors".

Recalling that His Power was released through the one hundred and twenty who had been praying together for nine days in obedience to their Lord's command, many people keep a "Prayer Vigil" at a Christian Ashram Retreat. I thank God for the faith and courage of those who several years ago in Sweden opened to me this wonderful door of adventure with Christ. Had I dreamed of what it would be, I might not have dared go; so perhaps it was just as well I did not realize that I was to lead the Ashram Retreat in the place of the great missionary, Dr. E. Stanley Jones, who at the last minute was unable to come. It was no accident that nine years before this I had come away from one of his five-day missions with the deep conviction: "If we supply the willingness to do His Will, God supplies the Power." So in this faith I went through each day, asking continuously, "Lord, let there be none of me and all of Thee all of the time."

It was humanly impossible that so much was done in so little time, but through this experience I came to know the meaning of "the anointing of the Spirit" and more than ever before, the grace of God who can use even a "broken straw". At the end of five days of speaking and counselling (all through interpreters) I found to my joy that the Holy Spirit had unified my talks with those given by the two Swedish pastors. Even though I had had no knowledge, other than charismatic, of their words because there had been no interpreting from Swedish into English, the Lord had proclaimed the same "message" through us all!

At the healing service, new to many that afternoon, we felt God's Healing Presence. As the pastor and I together laid our hands on each person who came to the altar rail, we prayed silently, "All of Thee, none of us, Lord", and aloud we alternated in thanking God for what He was doing in each one. A woman who had long ago lost her voice found it restored, to her great joy, and a skeptical nurse found that her leg was healed. A divided family found Christ together in a wonderful way. A young woman was instantly healed of mental illness, "re-born", and lived a month of spiritual growth on that, her first "birthday-in-the-Lord"; since then, she has witnessed to her family and to the doctor who had previously advised her, on leaving a mental hospital, to give up her religion! Many found physical healing, or peace of mind, forgiveness, and spiritual rebirth, according to their needs.

Over eighty persons—clergy, nurses, teachers and other lay people—had come to this retreat and most of them witnessed during a sharing period called "The Overflowing Heart" to what they had received from our Lord. God's Love so flooded all of us that miracles shone in their faces. But perhaps the greatest joy of all was the unity of spirit as Norwegians, Swedish and Finnish men and women, Methodists, Lutherans and others, joined with this lone American Episcopal laywoman in praising the Lord Jesus for His tidal wave of engulfing Love had made us one. As we parted, we sang "Blest Be The Tie That Binds Our Hearts In Christian Love"—and we knew that our fellowship had touched that of heaven!

At no time did Jesus state or imply that healing Love was the responsibility of only a chosen few. Even from a sacramental point of view, the laity have a very necessary part, for the priest must have a congregation before celebrating Holy Communion. The Church is not composed of ordained clergy alone; laity and clergy *together* make up the

Body of Christ.

The Christian parish is to be a family of concerned believers—those who have been ordained by baptism and confirmation into the *laos* or "people of God". The priest ministers to the laity and they in turn reach out to the community and the world about them. As a Spirit-filled fellowship of those who have had a genuine, transforming experience with Jesus Christ, the Church can bring the reality of Jesus as Living Lord to our troubled world that needs His healing and forgiveness. In its ministry of reconciliation, a parish church is an organism, not just an organization.

When will the Church become a place where all who enter its doors experience, through "the people of God", His reconciling, healing power and His unconditional, forgiving Love? When will Christians be truly "Christ-folk"—those in whom others sense the Love and Power of the Risen Christ? Our Lord has called each of us to be a member of His Body. No joy will supersede this adventure in His ministry of reconciliation. If we really love Him enough to commit our lives to His service, life will be a glorious walk with Jesus. Without Him, we cannot love ourselves or the world about us. He will use all of our personal suffering and the hard lessons that life has taught us, as well as our blessings, to prepare us to be instruments of His healing. It will be *His healing work through us!*

In *Total Prayer for Total Living,* Dr. Thomas A. Carruth writes of "The Beloved Community": " . . . we must have individuals who are channels of love and goodness, related to God in prayer, related to their fellow man in prayer, and related rightly to themselves in prayer. There is no substitute for this one in the structure and life of the Christian community. A thoroughly dedicated person who practices total prayer in this total life is one who is ever working, dreaming, loving, giving, and forgiving as a member of the community. He prays for his enemies, he prays with his friends, he prays with others about community concerns."[6]

We are called to become "the beloved Community". We need to have raised up among us a true "priesthood of all believers", not to take over the functions of the ordained ministry but to supplement them and thus extend their ministry of reconciliation. As the life of the human body flows out to the hand, so the Life of our Risen Lord should flow through His Body the Church and through each committed member who stretches forth a hand in compassion and in Christ's Name to touch the rejected, the sick, the wayward, the oppressed; to draw them also into the divine healing fellowship which is the purpose of the Church in the world. Will you be His hand extended in Love to those in need today? As you close this book, will you pray for the Lord to guide you to know and to do His Will?

To Him be the Glory, now and forever!

Recommended—Anne White's
new inspiring book
Dayspring
Published by Logos International

LIST OF SOURCES

The author is most grateful to the following publishers who have so kindly granted permission to quote from their publications. If, however, any copyright material has been used inadvertently, the author regrets the omission which will be corrected in any future edition of the book.

Unless otherwise stated, Bible references are taken by kind permission from *The New English Bible,* published by the Oxford University Press, and the Cambridge University Press, London, 1961.

Chapter I–MY FIRST ENCOUNTER
[1] Davey, Dr. T.F., "The Healing Ministry in the Mission of the Church" (London: *For Health and Healing,* Guild of Health, November-December, 1965) p. 170

Chapter II–WHAT IS DIVINE HEALING?
[1] Bennett, Dennis & Rita, *The Holy Spirit and You* (Plainfield, New Jersey: Logos International, 1971) Chapter 4

Chapter III–GOD'S WILL
[1] Evans, Dr. Griffith, *Cancer* (London: The Order of St. Luke the Physician in the United Kingdom, 1961; and Midland Bank Executor & Trustee Co., Ltd., Executors of author's estate) pp. 9, 11
[2] Carrel, Dr. Alexis, *Prayer Is Power* (Cincinnati, Ohio: The Forward Movement Publications–Reprint from *The Readers Digest)*
[3] Davey, Dr. T.F., "The Healing Ministry in the Mission of the Church" (London: *For Health and Healing,* Guild of Health, November-December, 1965) p. 169

Chapter V–HEALING THROUGH DOCTORS
[1] Wilson, Dr. Michael, "Looking Forward", *For Health and Healing,* Guild of Health (London: May, 1961) p. 10.
[2] Wilson, Dr. Michael, "Looking Forward", p. 10
[3] Evans, Dr. Griffith, *Cancer* (London: The Order of St. Luke the Physician in the United Kingdom, 1961; and Midland Bank Executor & Trustee Co., Ltd., Executors of author's estate) pp. 6, 7
[4] Evans, Dr. Griffith, *Cancer* (as above) p. 8
[5] Wilson, Dr. Michael, "Looking Forward", *For Health & Healing,* Guild of Health (London: May 1961) p. 10

Chapter VII–HEALING THROUGH MEANS OF GRACE
[1] Frost, Dr. Evelyn, *Christian Healing* (London: Guild of S. Raphael, 1954) p. 348
[2] *Prayer Book Studies III*–"The Order for the Ministration to the Sick" (New York: The Church Hymnal Corporation, 1951) pp. 6, 7
[3] *Book of Common Prayer* According to the Use of the Protestant Episcopal Church in the United States of America (New York: Oxford University Press, 1944) p. 320

Chapter IX—AVENUES TO HEALING

[1] Swaim, Dr. Loring T., *Arthritis, Medicine and the Spiritual Laws* (London: Blandford Press, Ltd., 1963) p. 9

[2] Johnson, The Rev. Ben Campbell, *Beyond Commitment* (Atlanta, Georgia: Spiritual Life Publishers, Inc., 1965) p. 95

Chapter X—BARRIERS TO HEALING

[1] Forget, Pastor Robert E., *The Way to Divine Healing* (London: Max Parrish and Co. Ltd., 1958) pp. 64, 65

[2] Johnson, The Rev. Ben Campbell, *Beyond Commitment* (Atlanta, Georgia: Spiritual Life Publishers, Inc., 1965) p. 82

Chapter XI—THE GIFTS OF THE SPIRIT

[1] Frost, Dr. Evelyn, *Christian Healing* (London: Guild of S. Raphael, 1954) p. 336

[2] Graham, Dr. Billy, *World Aflame* (Tadworth, England: World's Work Ltd. 1965) p. 82

Chapter XII—THE DELIVERANCE MINISTRY

[1] *Book of Common Prayer* According to the Use of the Protestant Episcopal Church in the United States of America (New York: Oxford University Press, 1944) p. 277

[2] *Book of Common Prayer* (as above) p. 278

[3] Bennett, Dennis & Rita, *The Holy Spirit and You* (Plainfield, New Jersey: Logos International, 1971) Chapter 4

[4] Harper, Michael, *Spiritual Warfare* (Plainfield, New Jersey, Logos International, 1970)

Chapter XIII—HEALING OF THE BODY OF CHRIST

[1] Palmer, The Rev. F. Noel, *The Pattern of Life in the Holy Communion* (London: Darton Longman & Todd Ltd., 1963) p. 68

[2] *Book of Common Prayer* According to the Use of the Protestant Episcopal Church in the United States of America (New York: Oxford University Press, 1944) p. 83

[3] *Book of Common Prayer* (as above) p. 82

[4] *Book of Common Prayer* (as above) p. 82

[5] *Book of Common Prayer* (as above) p. 83

[6] Carruth, Dr. Thomas A., *Total Prayer for Total Living* (Grand Rapids, Michigan: Zondervan Publishing House, 1962) pp. 93, 94